THE SOUTH CAROLINA BBQ PROJECT

Signs, symbols, and stories from the pit

Nathan Spainhour

Published by **Good Printed Things**

Written and Designed by Nathan Spainhour
Edited by Lelia King

First Edition

Printed in the United States of America
Good Printed Things
Greenville, South Carolina
goodprintedthings.com

ISBN: 979-8-9921993-5-2
LCCN: 2025950641

Image Use and Credits
All photographs are by the author unless otherwise
credited. Select images are reproduced under fair use
for commentary and historical context, with citations
provided. Images are reproduced for editorial and
documentary purposes; any individuals appearing are
shown in a documentary context and are not used for
commercial endorsement.

This project is funded in part by the Metropolitan
Arts Council which receives support from the City
of Greenville, BMW Manufacturing Company, and
SEW Eurodrive.

THE SOUTH CAROLINA BBQ PROJECT

CONTENTS

HOT BARBECUE

LOOK
PAST
THE
PLATE

FOREWORD

Robert F. Moss

The book you are holding is an exploration of
the visual culture of barbecue in South Carolina,
but it's more than just a feast for the eyes.
It takes us on a culinary tour of the Carolinas,
from the Upstate through the Midlands and into
the Pee Dee and Lowcountry. It delves into the
history and the many diverse flavors of the
state's rich barbecue tradition, tracing, as
Spainhour puts it, the "complex and winding
path of a cuisine."

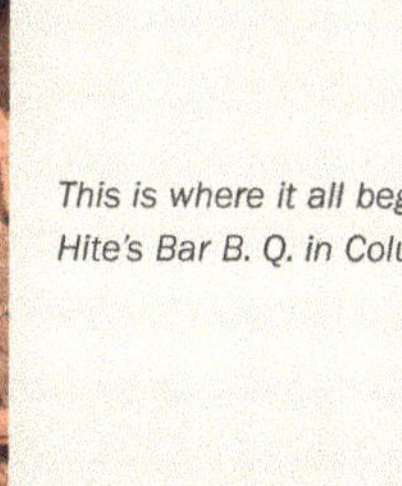

This is where it all begins.
Hite's Bar B. Q. in Columbia, South Carolina

There's plenty to explore, too, for South Carolina has one of the oldest and most complex traditions of any of America's great barbecue regions. Barbecue is indeed "the hub of a much larger wheel," to borrow Spainhour's phrase. You can't talk about it without delving into any number of other topics, like history, geography, race, and politics, to name just a few.

I might quibble with a few of the assertions found within the book. I would classify South Carolina, for instance, as being part of "the regular South" along with North Carolina and most of Virginia. For me, the Deep South starts somewhere south and west of Atlanta, but Spainhour's geography is a very "personal map of the South," as he freely admits in Part 1. This book is unapologetically personal in its outlook, which is exactly how it should be with barbecue.

A native of Anderson in the Upstate, Spainhour is adamant in his opinions, which are deeply rooted in the Palmetto State. He sees no need to explain that by "barbecue" he means pork, not smoked beef or barbecued chicken. While he notes in passing that a few states to our west have their own long-running barbe-cue traditions, he declares definitively that "anyone who knows anything about barbecue knows that it's North and South Carolina that is the heart of the institution." I won't argue with that.

It may be opinionated, but the *South Carolina BBQ Project* is finely attuned to the many nuances of the state's barbecue culture and to the evolving nature of that tradition. The text offers insightful delineations of the state's sub-regional variations and how they have evolved over time. From mustard sauce's recent migration far beyond its Midlands roots to the even more recent incursion of Texas-style brisket, Spainhour chronicles how old lines are blurring and oncet-distinct styles are coming together in the 21st century.

He doesn't shy away from the less savory side of the story, either. The book addresses head-on the dark side of industrial pork production in the 21st century and the legacy of Maurice Bessinger's Piggie Park restaurants in Columbia. There are plenty of more pleasant detours, too. Spainhour delves into South Carolina's somewhat mythic "Truth in Barbecue" law and the complex orthography of barbecue, including the distinction between the "garish and trashy 'q'" and the "upwardly mobile and buttoned-down 'c.'" (I will admit to being in the buttoned-down camp myself.)

Left: Making a detour to Easton Barbecue Co. in Hollywood, South Carolina
Right: "Rib Nite" sign at Elliott's BBQ Lounge painted by Denny Wesley in Florence, South Carolina

WE DELIVER!
bite
squad
Have your favorite dishes
delivered right to your door!
bitesquad.com
Welcome
BBQ
Catering
OPEN
OPEN
2401
yelp
Nextdoor
Neighborhood
Favorite
Nextdoor
Neighborhood
Favorite
Neighborhood
FAVE
nextdoor
Neighborhood
FAVE
nextdoor
FOOD GRADE RATING
Spectrum WiFi
Available Here
BUSINESS HOURS
We deliver with
DOORDASH
SMILE!
YOU'RE ON CAMERA

More than anything, this is a book about visual design. That starts with the design of the book itself. From the engaging color scheme—all reds, browns, and yellows—to the many maps, chapter ornaments, and graphical vignettes, the pages are as beautiful as they are stylish.

Spainhour has a keen eye for the visual nature of barbecue and what it means, be it the pig imagery used at barbecue restaurants to the typefaces on the signs and menus. The book explores how that imagery connects to the themes and connotations of barbecue and reflects the tension between nostalgia and the future.

I suspect that after reading this book you'll never look at South Carolina barbecue quite the same way again. I, for one, will no longer enter a barbecue joint without pausing first to assess the category in which its iconography belongs: "no pigs", "plain ole' pigs", "anthropomorphic pigs", or the somewhat disturbing "cannibal pigs."

I suspect, too, that reading this book will make you hungry enough to hit the road for a South Carolina barbecue tour of your own. It certainly had that effect on me.

It's the people, mostly men,
or all men, who are doing the work.
And I see them.

I see their sweat, and I see
their implements, and their shovel,
the very modest pits a lot of them use.

Fire, smoke — I mean, that's
what I see.

—Rien Fertel

The **MAJOR REGIONS** *of* **SOUTH CAROLINA**

In reality, the lines shown here are blurry. These divisions are generally agreed upon by those that live in the area, *generally* being the operative word. There are as many opinions about the landscape as there are about barbecue, which makes the indeterminate nature of these lines very appropriate.

INTRODUCTION

I don't remember the first time I ever had barbecue. In South Carolina, it's as ubiquitous as church and sweet tea. It's arguably been around since the Spanish came to shore here in the 1500s[1], and has been a part of the culture ever since. It may seem like a simple plate of food, but it carries the weight of memory, pride, and the kind of loyalty that draws lines on a map. I used to chalk it up to being in a similar emotional quadrant as football rivalries – lots of passion, but most fans (well, some fans) take a break once the season is over. Barbecue roots run deeper than that. Careers are made by it. Legacies are built on it. Regions are known for it. It's more than a cuisine, it helps define the culture.

---

1. This is a topic under debate. Barbecue has a few of those. I go into further detail later – but I just wanted you to know there is indeed a pin in this.

Just to be clear, when I'm talking about barbecue, I'm talking about pork – smoked over low heat for a long time – and that's all. I'll get into defining that in the pages to come, but I wanted to set the record straight before forging ahead.

Since I grew up in the South, I've always been around barbecue, but I wouldn't say I was immersed in it when I was young. That gave me just enough distance to study it with an outsider's perspective without being an outsider to the culture itself.

With that said, I'm not here to play referee in the "best barbecue" debate (I love Texas brisket too, but we're not talking about Texas). I wanted to dig deeper. I spent time researching the history, interviewing folks embedded in the culture, traveling across the state, and documenting the visual experience firsthand. This book is the result of that journey.

It's worth noting that this project began as a thesis for a master's degree in graphic design of all things. That might sound like an odd starting point, but through that research, I became deeply invested in the visual world surrounding barbecue – and, through it, the broader culture. One of the big takeaways? There's an incredible diversity in how barbecue is presented across South Carolina. The book is organized in a way that makes those variations easy to understand without getting so granular that the bigger picture gets lost.

South Carolina is divided into four regions, and this book follows that structure. Within each, at least one restaurant is explored as a case study. I document the visual culture – sharing my

Easter buffet at Elliott's BBQ Lounge. Whole hog barbecue presented on pig skin. Featuring a loaded buffet with every side you can imagine. Pork rinds and hushpuppies are shown here in addition to the pulled pork.

Smoked pork shoulder at the author's childhood home. We started this in the early morning and it took all day.

The Smokin' Pig is a barbecue restaurant in between Anderson and Clemson, South Carolina. The 'pig on fire' motif is one of many visual cues that is utilized in the identity of these establishments.

interpretations of the ephemera, the spaces, the people, and the food. By grounding the story in personal experiences, you'll get a stronger sense of what it feels like to visit these small but important places. Alongside the case studies, you'll also find essays exploring different aspects of the institution. Sometimes they are specific to the region, and other times they follow the logic of the overarching narrative. Together, they help tell a story of barbecue that's as layered and complex as the part of the country it calls home.

In designer George LaRou's essay "Roadside Culture: Visual Norms and How They Were Established," he states that:

" *Reviewing historic context allows us some deeper understanding of the interconnectivity of visual communication and cultural norms, and how each constantly informs and mutates the other.*[2]

I see this as a peek into a cuisine that's visual existence is layered with meaning – meaning that can easily go unnoticed unless you know what to look for. My goal is to be that of a translator[3], inter-preting what I've seen and sharing what I've come to understand.

To understand South Carolina barbecue, you have to understand the South. It's not only a craft – it's a lens into how this place tells its story, one plate at a time.

---

2. LaRou, George. *Roadside Culture: Visual Norms and How They Were Established*, 29
3. Sereina Rothenberger and David Scahtz of Hammer mentioned this in a 2019 presentation when talking about their collaborative work. Specifically, they said "we are but translators" – it stuck with me.

TODAY'S
SPECIALS

- Sweet Tea
- Southern Baptists
- Waffle House
- Civil War reenactmnt
- Grits
- Golf

CIRCLE M BBQ
HICKORY SMOKED
BBQ RIBS CHICKEN

I'M FROM THE SOUTH

Let's start with where I'm from – Anderson, South Carolina. It's in a part of the state that we call *the Upstate*. This includes pretty much the entire upper left corner of the triangle if you're looking at a map. Anderson is not a big town, but it's about two hours from Atlanta and two hours from Charlotte – right in the middle on Interstate 85. It's is a pretty conservative area with lots of small hamlets dotting the roads as you drive. It's definitely an area of back roads, the interstate doesn't do the landscape justice. I'm not sure if any interstate drive would do justice to any place.

Circle M BBQ on Highway 178 in Liberty, South Carolina

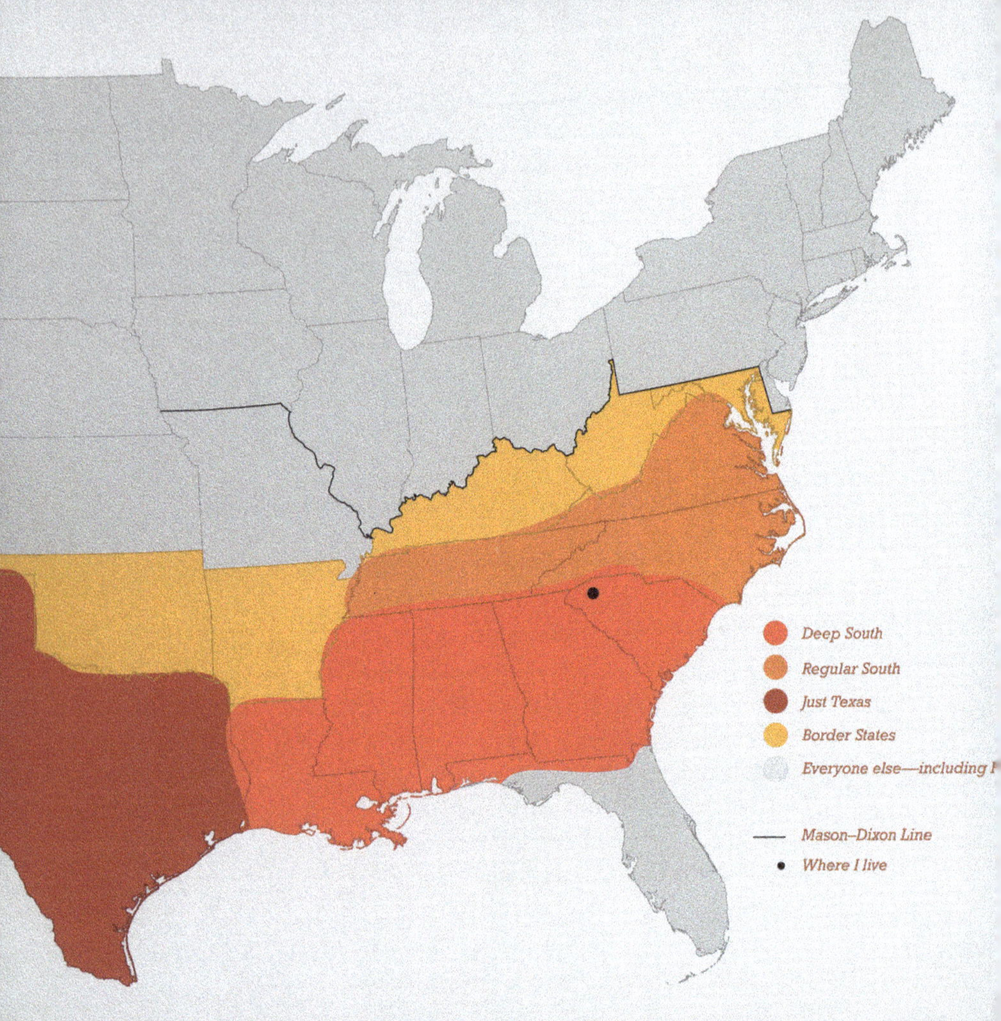

PERSONAL MAP
of the SOUTH

These are some of the major and minor regions of the South. A few are political boundaries, while others are just personal opinions. No matter what, if you ask someone in the next town over, they're likely to change everything that you see here.

Currently, I live in Greenville. It's half an hour up I-85 from Anderson. Greenville is an old mill town. During the first half of the 20th century it was known as the "textile center of the South" due to its hosting of the Southern Textile Exposition for 45 years straight.[4] Most of the textile business has moved away, but the area was smart in its thinking about how the town grew. There's a good bit of diversity in the types of companies that have invested here which has kept things afloat during the many recessions since the heyday of textiles. We have a BMW plant in the area, Michelin's North American headquarters is here, GE makes wind turbines near Woodruff Road, and my wife works at a Fortune 100 IT distributor with a major office in town. Not to mention, I landed my first design job at one of the largest power tool manufacturers in the world (which incidentally is up the road from my house).

Needless to say, the area is doing okay from an economic perspective. I think it may be because of this influx of business – and all of the out-of-towners coming in for their respective companies – that Greenville is slowly becoming more

4. Wilkerson, *Slow Travels-North Carolina and South Carolina*, 143

progressive in one of the more conservative parts of the state. It's interesting living only thirty minutes from where you grew up and feeling like you're on a different planet when it comes to how people view the world. The locals are used to newcomers at this point, but they're not always thrilled about it. Most complaints center around the traffic. My feeling? It could be worse. This place is growing fast.

So, why barbecue?

It is the hub of a much larger wheel. When you talk about barbecue, you can't help but talk about the South. And when you talk about major influences that the South has contributed to the overall culture, barbecue would certainly be on that list. South Carolina has a deep history with the cuisine, and the visual culture surrounding it is a lens that reveals a larger story. This culture showcases commonalities between all of us, as well as some stark regional differences. All of which help define South Carolina culture as a whole, and sometimes directly mirrors society. There's not much that can't be talked about through the lens of smoked pork, but diving straight into what sides you would like with your sandwich is irresponsible without a little more historical context.

The order counter at Midway BBQ in Buffalo, South Carolina. Note that the list of sides is written with marker on a long sheet of paper.

SET THE RECORD STRAIGHT

BARBECUE: A BRIEF HISTORY

It's pretty amazing how cuisine can be so intertwined with culture. This is definitely the case with barbecue in the South. It seems to have many rumored origins, but what I have gathered is that the word was derived from a frame of green sticks used for cooking by the Taino Indians in the Caribbean – baribicu. This became barbacoa in Spanish and barbecue in English. Native Americans also cooked meat in this fashion. The original idea of a pit came from that culture – although they used it for storage as well as for cooking.[5]

5. Moss, *Barbecue Lovers of the Carolinas*, 7

How they cook their fish, 1590. Bry, Theodor De, Engraver, and John White, courtesy of the Library of Congress Rare Book and Special Collections Division (LC-USZ62-53339)

The low and slow pork didn't happen until the 1500s when pigs were introduced to the North American continent by the Spanish. That's where the style of cooking was married with the hog, and history was made. There is definitely some contention about where this happened exactly, but for the purpose of this narrative, all that really matters is understanding how the first real American cuisine came to be.[6]

By the 18th and 19th centuries, it had become common to hold barbecue events around the South. Politicians weren't campaign-

6. There is a hotly contested debate on whether barbecue as I'm describing it started in the Spanish settlement of Santa Elena (now Parris Island) South Carolina or up the east coast a bit more. Mainly, we're focusing on when pigs were introduced to the cooking scene in North America. Some argue that it was when the Spanish brought the first hogs onto the South Carolina coast that the first real barbecue was produced. Others argue that the evidence of those hogs actually getting cooked in this way is thin, and that it may have happened later or further north. Things we can agree on? It happened on the eastern seaboard – and it was as much a credit to Native Americans as it was the Europeans.

ing unless they hosted a barbecue for their constituents – they were a staple in American politics at the very beginning. George Washington "recorded attending six such events between 1769 and 1774, including, on September 18, 1773, 'a Barbicue [sic] of my own giving at Accotinck.'"[7] Andrew Jackson, however, was the first president to host a barbecue at the White House in 1829. The idea of a barbecue was so prevalent in politics, it was used in a political cartoon skewering (pun intended) Jackson, complete with cloven hoof, over the coals of "public opinion."

In the 19th century, it was common for enslaved individuals working on plantations to orchestrate barbecues for holidays and special occasions.

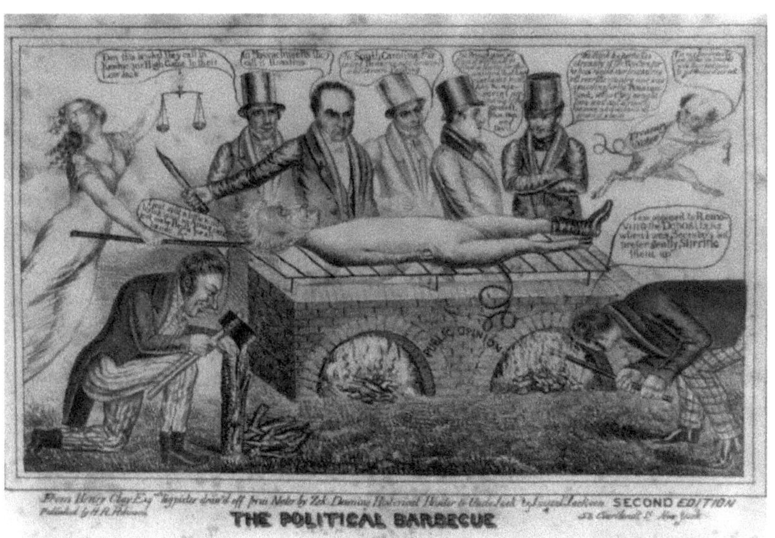

The Political Barbecue, 1834. Lithograph by Henry R. Robinson, courtesy of the Library of Congress, Prints & Photographs Division (LC-DIG-ds-14739)

7. Moss, *Barbecue, The History of an American Institution*, 13

Robert Moss writes about Fredrick Douglass' take on the holidays, saying they were:[8]

These events actively occurred right up to the start of the Civil War in the 1860s. Despite being used as a form of oppression by plantation owners, the skills developed around the pits by the enslaved workers would benefit them in years to come. After the war, June 19th came to be known as Emancipation Day, and communities across the South often marked it with barbecue.

During Reconstruction, migration into larger towns and cities helped carry these traditions forward. Formerly enslaved people, laborers, and entrepreneurs all contributed to the formation of regional barbecue styles as the cuisine found new homes across the South and beyond. As Moss notes,

" *Today's barbecue cultures in cities such as Houston, Memphis, St. Louis, Kansas City, and Chicago have their roots in the Emancipation Day and July Fourth celebrations of the Reconstruction Days.*[9]

Mostly, the word "barbecue" had been used to refer to an event up to this point. It didn't start becoming a specific type of cuisine until the early 20th century. One thing that it is not, is a grill.

Be prepared to get your hand slapped if you start referring to your Weber gas grill as being a barbecue. That's a no-no. Barbecue is smoked meat. That's it. There's enough variation available in those four words already – no need to throw a whole other variable into the mix.

8. In this caption, Robert Moss is quoting from the book *Narrative of the Life of Frederick Douglass (1845)*. Douglass was a 19th century abolitionist who helped end slavery through his writings about himself having been enslaved before escaping to the North. Moss, *Barbecue, The History of an American Institution*, 68

9. Moss, *Barbecue, The History of an American Institution*, 102

"Not a custom of benevolence but rather 'the most effective means in the hands of the slaveholder in keeping down the spirit of insurrection' and 'part and parcel of the gross fraud, wrong, and inhumanity of slavery'...Douglass notes that many masters not only allowed slaves to get drunk during holidays but actively encouraged it through drinking contests and the means. In Douglass' view, this was not a form of entertainment but a means of enforcing control."

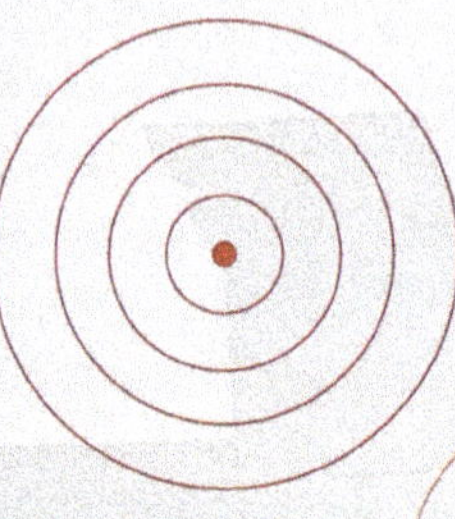
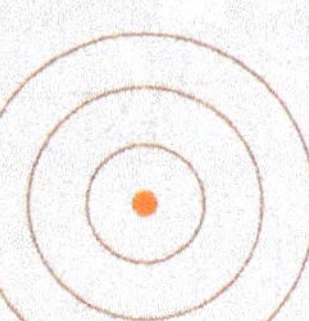
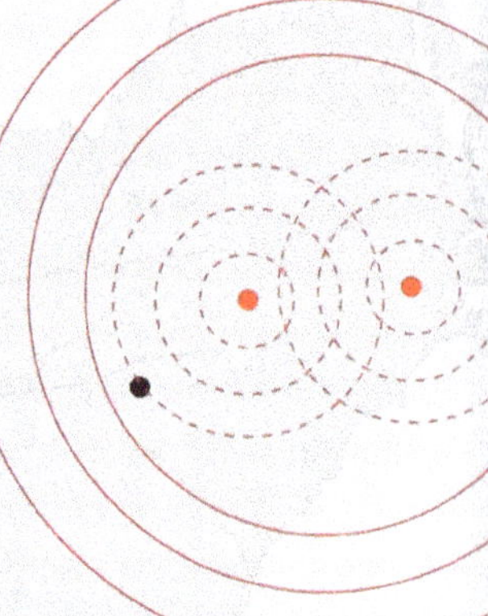
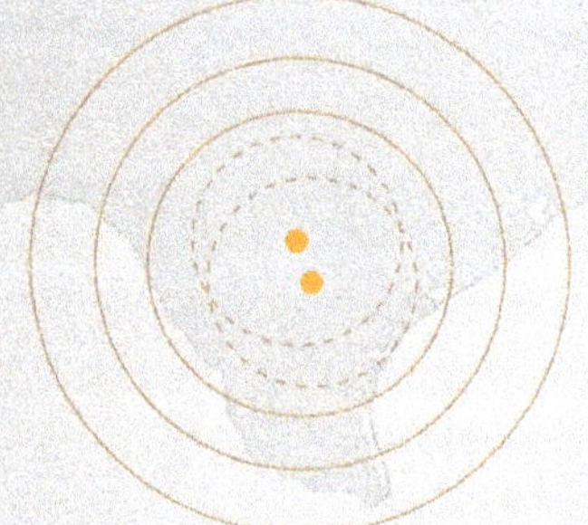

● **Kansas City, MO**
Known as one of the main barbecue capitals in the U.S. The Kansas City Barbeque Society set the standard for barbecue contest judging in America.

● **Memphis, TN**
Home of the blues and some dang good barbecue. Memphis was a migration hub during Reconstruction, and holds the claim as the originator of the barbecue sandwich.

● **Where I live**

❋ **Every state that has real barbecue**

● **Lockhart and Austin, TX**
Texas rides their own bull when it comes to barbecue. It's very different than the pork-centric variety of the South. If you want some slow-cooked brisket or anything pretty much beef related, this area is unmatched.

● **Lexington and Ayden, NC**
The epicenter of Southern barbecue. Vinegar and pepper in the east and a touch of tomato in the west (or Piedmont). The James Beard Foundation awarded a BBQ restaurant in each of these cities in the same year so as not to rock any cultural boats.

MAJOR BBQ REGIONS *in the* UNITED STATES

This is where the battle lines are drawn. By no means is this a comprehensive map of major barbecue regions. It just points out well known areas, their general range of influence, and what they're known for. You can get about as granular as the Burgundy region of France if you want to. Notably, South Carolina is not one of them. That is changing.

This leads us to barbecue as we think of it today. It has become a dish that is mainly cooked in the southern United States. Many other states put on a show at trying to do it, but they just don't get it. Just like France and its wine regions, there are major regions for barbecue – each one famous for its own contribution to the cuisine. This subdivision of regions was established once barbecue restaurants began to take shape.[10] This is also a big reason why barbecue has become an institution. Each region is now adamant about their version of the dish and will staunchly defend it to their graves.

The real battle for the origins of barbecue as we know it – whole hog – is between North and South Carolina. The eastern parts of each state practice the art of whole-hog cooking. Many places focus on the fatty shoulder (or use the ham), and while that makes a tasty sandwich, the whole-hog is a more complex process that produces a nuanced final product. These two regions use a vinegar and pepper mixture to cook with and are the grandparents of barbecue culture. You'll hear Texas (the state), Kansas City, and Memphis all beat their chest over their wares, but anyone who knows anything

10. It was kind of a slow build. Barbecue stands began to appear on roadsides and they morphed into what you may now call restaurants as they became more permanent. Moss, *Barbecue, The History of an American Institution*, 129-130

about barbecue knows that it's eastern North and South Carolina that is the heart of the institution. I have no opinion on which region started barbecue – I just know that the area I live in makes some of the best of it in the world.

Since I live in South Carolina, I'm going to focus here. This is the only state that has four official sauces: vinegar and pepper, heavy tomato, light tomato, and mustard.[11] I've witnessed non-South Carolinian barbecue enthusiasts shun the mustard variety, but it's one of my favorites – right alongside vinegar and pepper. Mustard runs mainly through the Midlands and traces back to the early German settlers in the region.[12] Up in the area where I live, where heavy tomato supposedly dominates, you'll still find all four sauces in just about any establishment you visit.

At the beginning of this research, I had a theory about the barbecue restaurants scattered around the Upstate: the more ramshackle the place – the more homemade the sign or logo – the better the food inside. I've since learned that this isn't always true, but the search led me to the South Carolina Barbecue Association (SCBA) and their restaurant rankings.

11. Kovacik and Winberry, *South Carolina: The Making of a Landscape*, 209
12. Moss, *Barbecue Lover's The Carolinas*, 110

SOUTH CAROLINA
SAUCE REGIONS
Circa 1989

Heavy tomato
Light tomato
Mustard
Vinegar and pepper

The areas represented by the sauces on
this map are referencing a study conducted
in "South Carolina: The Making of a Landscape,"
a research project by professor Charles F.
Kovacik of the University of South Carolina.
This is innacurate now since the sauces are
pervasive everywhere, but it still offers a sense
of where they may have originated.

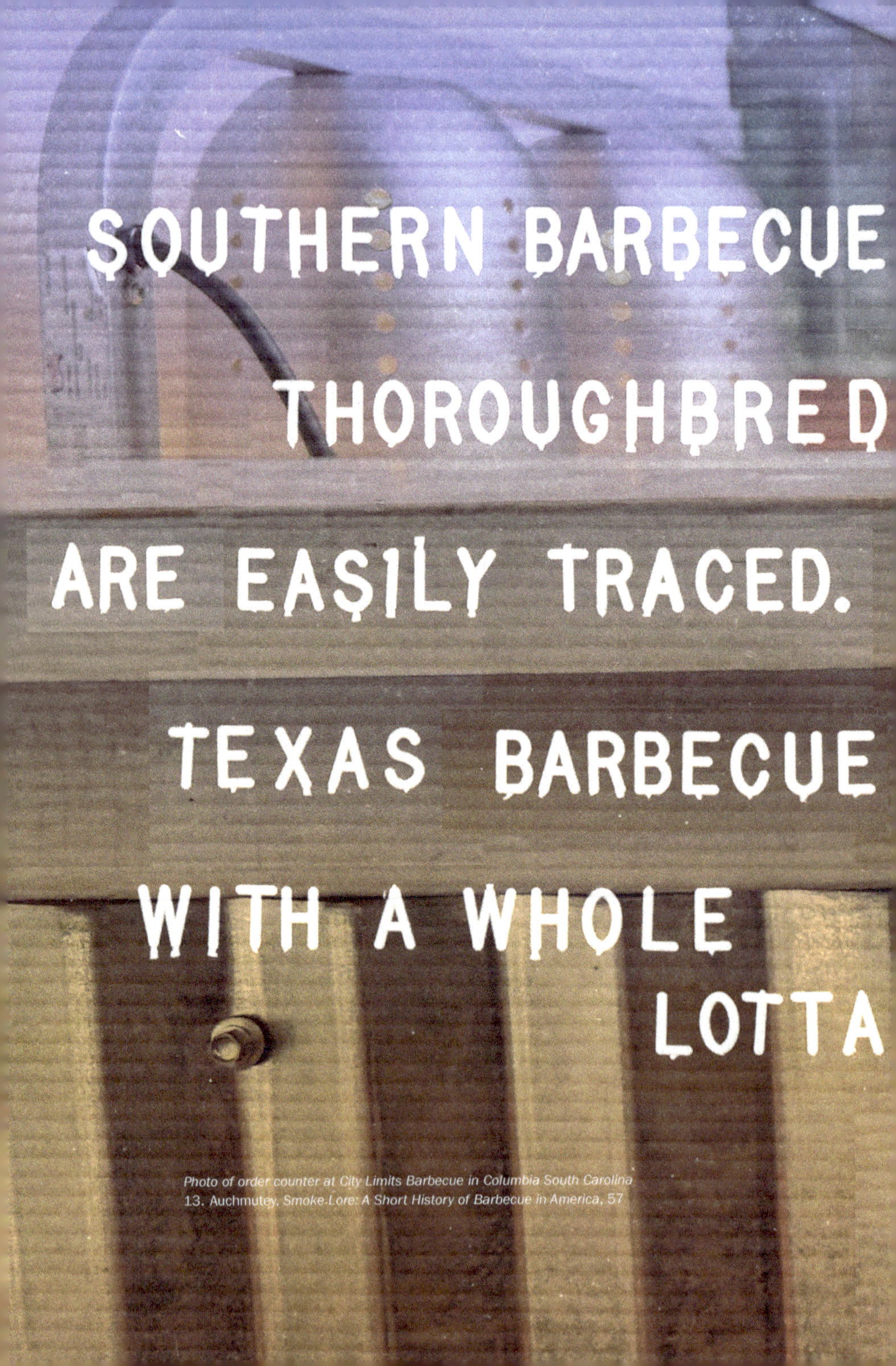

SOUTHERN BARBECUE THOROUGHBRED ARE EASILY TRACED. TEXAS BARBECUE WITH A WHOLE LOTTA

Photo of order counter at City Limits Barbecue in Columbia South Carolina

13. Auchmutey, *Smoke-Lore: A Short History of Barbecue in America*, 57

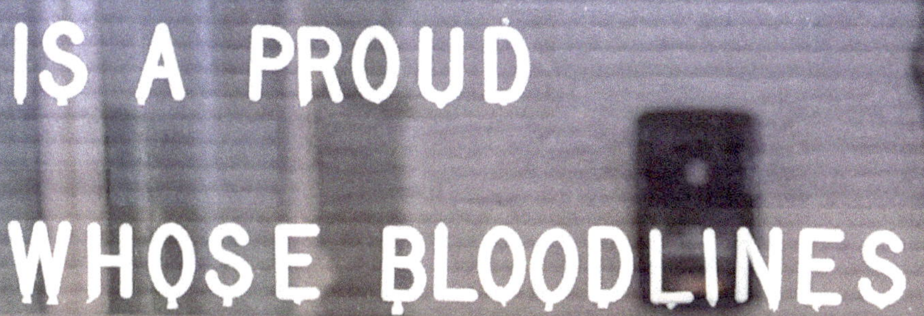

IS A PROUD

WHOSE BLOODLINES

IS A FEISTY MUTT

CRAZY RELATIVES.
- ROB WALSH

MEATS
TEXAS BEEF RIB (AVE. WEIGHT 1.3LBS)
TEXAS BRISKET (SLICED OR CHOPPED)
PIT SMOKED PORK
PULLED
CHOPPED w/ PIEDMONT STYLE "CHOP SAUCE" VINEGAR
CHOPPED w/ CRISPY SKINS w/Chop Sauce
SPARE RIBS (PORK, SALT ONLY, COOKED OVER COALS)
PORK BELLY BURNT ENDS (CHAR SIU)
SMOKED WINGS (8)
SMOKED HALF-CHICKEN

SANDWICHES   SERVED ON A PREMIUM BRIOCHE BUN
BRISKET SANDWICHES
CHOPPED
MEXICANO
BRISKET + PICKLED RED ONIONS + SWEET PICKLED JALAPENOS + TEXAS F
PIT SMOKED PORK BBQ SANDWICHES
PULLED sauce choice on side
CHOPPED (dressed w/ Chop Sauce)
CHOPPED w/ CRISPY SKINS w/ Chop Sauce
CAROLINA DRESSED w/ CHOP SAUCE + Sweet Jalap

The SCBA[14] once listed two main categories of barbecue joints on their website: the "100-Mile Barbecue" establishments – so good that it would be worth driving 100 miles to eat there – and the "Worth-the-Trip" runners-up. The list was never exhaustive, but it provided a starting point for exploring the state's best-known pits. Today, that same list (along with dozens more restaurants) lives on the Destination BBQ website (a labor of love by Heather and Jim Roller), a comprehensive South Carolina barbecue directory that's been quietly keeping the flame alive. The SCBA list may not be updated as often as it once was, but it remains one of the best resources for finding excellent barbecue.[15]

One thing that's remained consistent, though, is how these restaurants show up online. Many still rely more on social media than on traditional websites – sometimes skipping a site altogether, or using their Destination BBQ profile as a kind of stand-in homepage. A few have invested in full-fledged sites, but they're still the minority. I suspect the hesitation comes down to the usual mix of cost, time, and the feeling that their profile "does enough." To be fair, many of these restaurants have been around for decades, with regulars lining up each week – proof that a sandwich post or tailgate special shared to followers can work just fine. Honestly, some of them still feel like secrets, and selfishly, I'd kind of like to keep it that way.

14. In every major barbecue region there is typically an organization like the SCBA that is perfectly attuned to their particular type of barbecue. Many have strict standards, and South Carolina has some of the most highly trained barbecue judges in the country. Another book could be written solely focused on the competition circuit where the judges make their rounds. In fact, it's not unusual for pitmasters to start restaurants after they perfom well at one of these events.

15. Heather and Jim Roller, *Destination BBQ*, https://destination-bbq.com

THE
UPSTATE

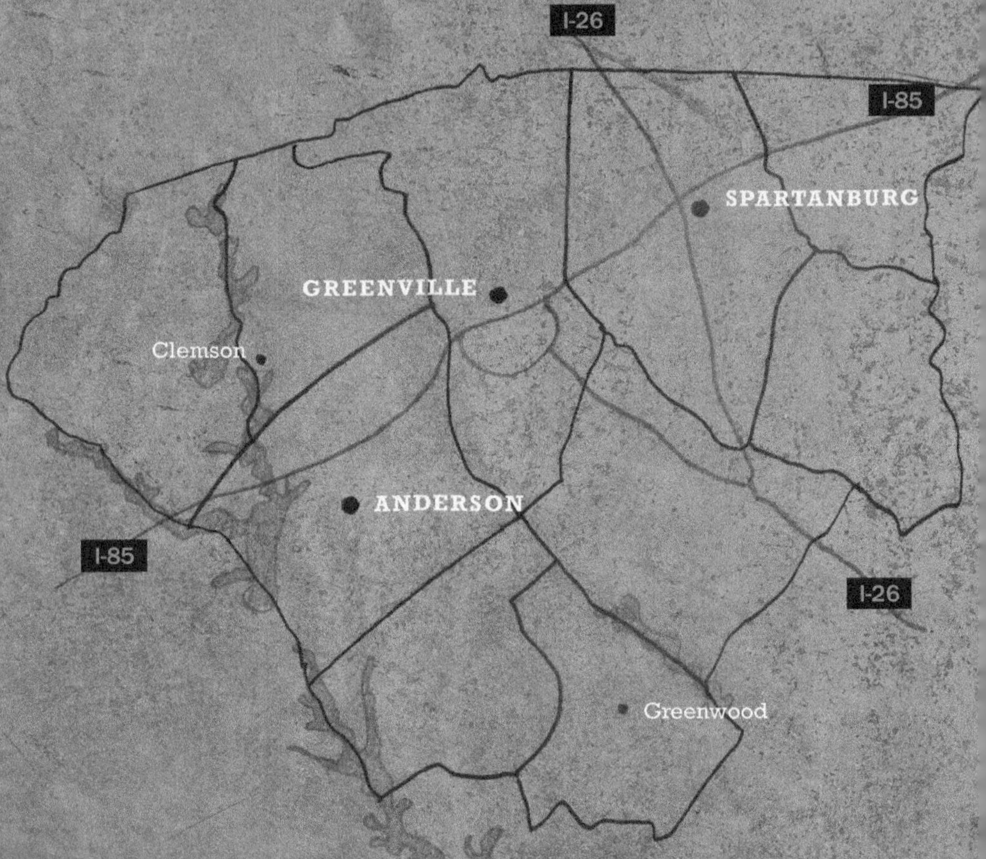

The UPSTATE REGION
of SOUTH CAROLINA

The major cities are marked here, along with a few smaller towns worth noting. Greenville is the biggest and has some excellent barbecue, but you'll be rewarded if you venture off the main highways. Around here, hidden gems are everywhere.

OVERVIEW

The Upstate of South Carolina is made up of ten counties –
Greenville is the largest from a population perspective, and
Spartanburg is second. Anderson is third down the list but I
think due to its distance from Interstate 85 – and possibly lack
of interest in growth – it never grew as large as the other two.[16]
This is pure speculation on my part, but I feel like I can do that
since I grew up there. Clemson University is the agriculturally
focused state school – located in Pickens. Gaffney, famous for
the big peach water tower on I-85, is located in Cherokee. The
other counties are pretty rural, similar to much of the state.

The Upstate is also sometimes referred to as the Piedmont,
and we're apparently known for tomato-based barbecue sauces.[17]
As I mentioned earlier, every restaurant that I visited had three to
four sauces, and mustard sauce was always present. Since South
Carolina is known for the mustard sauce from the Midlands, it
may seem a little inauthentic to anyone from out-of-town if it
wasn't present, no matter where they were in the state.

---

16. Census.gov 2019 estimates of the population of each city are as follows:
    Greenville – 70,635, Spartanburg – 37,399, and Anderson – 27,676. The
    county population probably reflects the density more accurately since this is
    definitely an area of the country that grows out and not up: Greenville County –
    523,542, Spartanburg County – 319,785, and Anderson County – 202,558.
17. This runs into the Piedmont region of North Carolina as well. Western North
    Carolina, not including the mountains, is considered the Piedmont.

HOG
HEAVEN

CASE STUDY

HENRY'S SMOKEHOUSE

In his book *The One True Barbecue*, Rien Fertel writes, "South Carolinians have always been partial to a handful of barbecue dynasties, mini fiefdoms that operate under the same name."[18] There are probably more than a few reasons why this happens, not a minor one being that once you're in, you're in. Locals don't trust outsiders much – that's been changing over the years – but I imagine this still holds true when it comes to barbecue.

Another reason is that the job is hard work. Most proprietors' "pits are open source"[19] as the people that have the stamina and patience to do it for a living are few and far between, so

18. Fertel, *The One True Barbecue*, 157
19. Fertel, *The One True Barbecue*, 150

they're not afraid of the competition stealing their secrets. Well, that is except for their sauce recipes – that's something they'll guard with their life. All of that taken into consideration though, the thought of a child taking over for their parent in the family business, as romantic of an idea as it is, is considerably easier said than done. There are definitely places it works out – take the Bessingers or the Scotts in the lower regions of the state – but more often than not, it's safe to say that unless the barbecue restaurant has an heir apparent or an expansion plan, it will probably close down after the owner doesn't feel like working anymore.

In a conversation I had with Robert Moss, foremost historian on the subject, he emphasized this trend:

Because of this, Upstate barbecue is unlike other parts of the state, in that it's still all pretty new, comparatively speaking. Most of these places didn't appear until the 1990s, with some exceptions. There aren't many legacies to build on or histories to contend with. They started with a clean slate – sort of. I think of the Upstate as the middle child when it comes to South Carolina barbecue. The Pee Dee and Midlands share the title of the oldest sibling, and the Lowcountry is the youngest.[20] The Upstate has new barbecue blood and doesn't seem tied to long-standing regional traditions, but it's not so new that everyone wants to reinvent the cuisine. In fact, some of the modern barbecue restaurants in Charleston have opened outposts here. More and more, the regions are bleeding together.

20. This is kind of a funny statement considering how old Charleston is. There is certainly a large presence of South Carolina barbecue history in the Lowcountry but, the legacies that I speak of aren't necessarily rooted there.

"It's the thing about upstate barbecue, that scene has just almost turned over. There's the Little Pigs – there used to be several Little Pigs in Greenville. There's one left. All the places in Greenville like Henry's, and Mike and Jeff's, and Mutt's. None of those places were there when I was living in Greenville. I moved down to Columbia in '92, and then started exploring all the Midlands' places, most of which are still there [today]."

HENRY'S
SHOKEHOUSE

Henry's Smokehouse is a prime example of an Upstate icon.
I live in the city of Greenville, and it's about a six-minute drive
from my house. Not long ago this area of town was pretty
nondescript. I remember a shopping center anchored by a dry
cleaner across the street from the restaurant. There was also
a brutalist building a block away housing an insurance company.
Now, there's a fancy grocery store next door (blocking the view
of the insurance building), complete with integrated apartments.
The shopping center still has the dry cleaner, but it also has a
popular local coffee shop. The new anchor is Community Tap, a
neighborhood favorite craft beer and wine bar. These additions
have drawn a new subset of people to this part of town and
Henry's has stayed exactly the same – and is thriving.

It was the perfect place to go for lunch on a crisp fall day when
the smoke from the pits cut through the air enough to lure me
off the road and into the parking lot. The sign on the street had
what looked to be hand cut, rounded serif, wooden letters that
spell out:

HENRY'S SMOKEHOUSE

in dark green over a white field. There's a little shingled roof on
top of the sign too, making it a look like a tiny house elevated
above the sidewalk.

Henry's is the ideal location to catch any visitor to our tourist-
friendly town trying to get a taste of a local specialty. It came
on the scene in 1991 and serves hickory coal-smoked Boston
Butt all week, not just on the weekend like many other barbecue
establishments.

I got out of my car and walked in one of two doors on either side of the restaurant – it probably seats 25 people. The building is set off the street with picnic tables out front and a dining room wrapped on three sides by glass. I read that it was an old general store before Beau Hammond bought it and transformed it into a smokehouse.[21] Tiger O'Rourke (who started as a dishwasher at Henry's in college) and Bo Wilder are the current owners, and have kept everything true to the original.

21. Moss, *Barbecue Lover's The Carolinas*, 159

Inside the restaurant, a counter stretched against the back wall. The only window on this side looked into the kitchen, and the smoking metal pits were further towards the back of the building. This counter is where I ordered my lunch. There was wood paneling all over – on the walls, the counter, and even the outside of the restaurant had the outdoor-friendly kind. It's like a true smokehouse shack mixed with a 50s drive-in diner due to all of the glass. Henry's is the perfect place to enjoy a sandwich, and honestly has an aesthetic about it that new restaurants might try to emulate for their social-media savvy clientele.

Images from previous iterations of the menu above the counter show it as a white board with black neutral sans-serif text printed directly on it. There used to be two decorative elements. The first was a border of what looked like actual currency from around the world stapled to the wall, kind of a subtle way to showcase the international clientele of the Upstate. The second was an image of an anthropomorphic pig with black sunglasses. He was in the center-bottom of the menu presiding over the cashiers. The pig was staring straight at the viewer and was positioned as if he was leaning up against a bar, smiling.

The current menu board has done away with the dollar bills and the pig, unfortunately. The mascot does still appear in other places around the restaurant, including the ubiquitous styrofoam cups. These cups are a common fixture – they hold crushed ice and help keep the drinks cold.

I ordered a barbecue plate with hash and rice and potato salad.[22] After I paid, I found myself in a common fast-casual conundrum – the one where you need to wait for your food before you sit down.

---

22. These are some really traditional sides in South Carolina barbecue. The potato salad is a part of what's known as the holy trinity, and hash and rice is a conversation unto itself. I go into all of this a bit later.

HOG HEAVEN
www.henryssmokehouse.com
D 1007 • Woodruff Road 864-213-9770
HOME OF THE
HENRY'S
SMOKEHOUSE
LEANEST BUTT IN TOWN!
Wade Hampton 864-232-7774 • Simps

Some people don't do this. The biggest faux pas here is skipping the line and sitting down while someone else orders for you – unless you've got small kids in tow or you're with folks who have trouble standing for long stretches. That move can leave people holding plates of food with nowhere to eat, while others with no food at all take up table space. That's never fun. Luckily, most people seem to understand the delicate timing that keeps the seats turning.

I decided to make good use of my time while I waited, and poured myself a mixture of sweet and unsweet tea. This is what I do when I want to justify the completely empty calories – it's so good.

You see a lot of sweet tea as a staple beverage throughout the state – and lemonade. Cheerwine is a cherry-flavored soda from North Carolina that you can find in local establishments. In the Pee Dee region, Red Rock Strawberry Soda is the way to go.[23] Smaller barbecue establishments never have been places that you would typically find alcohol, at least in my lifetime. That's changing now in some of the newer establishments, but Henry's keeps it dry.

On the opposite side of the cup that features the pig in sunglasses is the more formal seal of a logo. It is a woodcut in the shape of a circle. Henry's Smokehouse is in small caps set in the same typeface as the sign out front – it breaks the border. There is a scene of a log cabin below the name that is completely enclosed within the circle. The tag line "home of the

23. Gidick, *Top Chefers should have followed Robert Moss' Top 10 Barbecue Commandments.* It is no small feat to find the Red Rock strawberry soda. The closest place that I could buy it is three hours away in Florence, SC.

leanest butt in town!" is set in a western slab serif, and wraps
around the diameter. This is bringing attention to what makes
Henry's barbecue a favorite: hand-pulled pork, with as little fat
as possible being served.

The wood block Antique typefaces connote a feeling of the Wild
West saloons one would see in TV shows like Deadwood or films
like Once Upon a Time in the West. The serif type reminds me of
the woodblock letterpress "Wanted" posters from the 19th and
early 20th century.[24] This is a common motif in barbecue restaurant branding in the Upstate and Midlands (and elsewhere).

These letterforms became popular in the decades after Reconstruction, as America's visual language evolved alongside its
shifting social landscape. Wood type had begun to be mass-pro-
duced (rather than hand-carved) in the 1820s and grew in pop-
ularity throughout the nineteenth century, shaping the look of
posters, broadsides, and other large-scale signage and printed
materials. By the early twentieth century – around the time of
the Great Migration, when Southern culture and cuisine began
moving northward – its large letterforms, clear hierarchy, and
decorative slab-serifs reigned supreme. The visual dominance
of these letterforms, combined with the mythology of the frontier
and imagery of cowboys cooking over open flames, may have
contributed to the style's enduring association with barbecue.
A pig roasting over fire remains one of its most common and
recognizable depictions.

When my order was ready at the counter, I took the styrofoam
covered tray outside to one of the picnic tables. The straw in my
styrofoam cup crunched on the crushed ice. I'm always careful

 24. Shields, *What Is Wood Type?*

Unsweet and sweet tea at Henry's.

with cups like this as I remember when I was young driving the straw through the side wall and spilling soda all over the place. Nevertheless, the cup is sturdy and would frankly feel strange if it were the paper variety.

I always start eating barbecue as is – it's one of those tests to see if it's of a high quality. If it can stand on its own with no additional sauce, you've found a winner. This pork did not disappoint. If you want to try sauces with it though, Henry's has three different choices: a mild tomato, spicy tomato, and a spicy mustard. As I mentioned earlier, mustard has spread far beyond its Midlands roots, and spots like Henry's reflect that. Some folks call it homogenization, and others see it as a simple matter of giving customers what they expect. Either way, mustard has become part of the statewide landscape. Personally, I love vinegar and pepper sauce and mustard sauce equally – it depends on where I'm eating and my mood. The barbecue at Henry's is some of the best in the Upstate. It's not whole-hog, but it is cooked over wood coals, it's really tasty, and it's an example of how the restaurants of this region don't feel the need to hold to a particular style to be relevant.

As I sat outside at one of the picnic tables trying not to drip sauce on myself, I noticed the Hog Hauler parked nearby. That's the name of Henry's food truck (and its mobile billboard). One trait I enjoy about many local barbecue restaurateurs is their shameless use of tongue-in-cheek messaging. There's a folksy quality to the humor and visuals – an unpolished sincerity that's hard to pull off unless you really mean it. Many of the smaller joints share this attitude, and it creates a distinct tone within the industry that perpetuates the down-home, no-nonsense vibe that runs through it.

Since Henry's has more than one location, it could qualify as a chain, but it's not your typical fast-food operation. It's a business that has managed to grow while still holding on to its local credentials – something that's hard to do in barbecue. If Henry's can keep its people and its quality strong, I could see it becoming a kind of mini-fiefdom in the Upstate.

In the meantime, I'll keep coming back to this location – sometimes on my own, sometimes with out-of-town friends – not just for the food, but for the feeling that some things don't need reinventing. Henry's keeps doing what it has always done: slow-smoked pork over wood coals, served without pretense. In a town that's constantly shifting, there's something comforting about a place that stays true to itself.

PLATES
All Plates Served with 2 Sides
Regular Sandwich Plate $10.25
Hog Sandwich Plate $11.00
Chopped Pork Plate $11.00
Smoked Chicken Plate $10.25
Combination Plates
Pork, Chicken, Ribs
Choice of any 2 $16.75
Choice of any 3 $18.00
Henry's Ribs ½ Rack $16.45
Henry's Ribs Full Rack $27.45
Hash and Rice $10.25

SIDES
Beans $2.25
Slaw $2.25
Potato Salad $2.25
Green Beans $2.25
Sweet Potato Casserole $2.25
Macaroni and Cheese $2.25
French Fries $2.75
Hash and Rice $6.75
Brunswick Stew $6.75
Rice $1.10
Peach Cobbler $2.75
Chips (Plain or BBQ) $1.25

HENRY'S SMOKEHOUSE
Catering for All Occasions
Low Country Boils - Oyster Roast - Fish Fries

DRINKS
Iced Tea and Soft Drinks $2.25
Tea by the Gallon $6.00

DESSERTS
Banana Pudding Side $2.00
Banana Pudding Pint $6.75
Cakes, Cookies, Brownies $2.00

SAUCES
Mild or Spicy
Bottle - $3.75   Gallon - $25.00

SANDWICHES
Regular $6.50
Hog $7.75
Hash, Small $6.50
Hash, Large $7.75
Smoked Chicken $6.50

BULK
Chopped Pork
$7.75 ½ LB $14.75 LB
Hash
$7.75 ½ LB $14.75 LB
Smoked Chicken
$7.75 ½ LB $14.75 LB
Henry's Ribs
$13.75 ½ RACK $24.00 FULL RACK
Beans, Slaw, Green Beans,
Potato Salad
$3.99 ½ LB $5.50 LB
Sweet Potato Casserole
$4.50 ½ LB $7.50 LB
Macaroni and Cheese
$4.50 ½ LB $7.50 LB
Brunswick Stew
$8.00 Pint
Peach Cobbler
$4.75 LB

Tailgate
2 # pork OR chicken
4 Sides
gallon of tea
Dozen Buns
$62.50

CANNIBALISM
& YOUR BRAND

DIG THE PIG

Using a pig as a logo for a barbecue joint is definitely cliché, but in terms of capturing the tone of the cuisine – and the people that make it – I can't argue with the choice. There's something to be said about being direct about what you're selling. It's as straight-forward as smoking a pig over low heat for hours on end.

The following pages show some of the more interesting uses of the pig as an identity element.[25]

25. The images featured over the following pages were mostly taken by me. The ones that aren't, were gathered from the online presence of the establisments represented. There was no photo credit for them, but I have noted the information that I was able to acquire.

One branch of the
pork-as-identity family tree
is the personification of
the pigs themselves.

What is really fascinating
is how seemingly happy they
all are. It's a strange sentiment,
mascots as cannibals.

Midway BBQ is a strong example of the pig used in conjunction with the shortened "BBQ" to create a logomark.[26]

If a restaurant has an animal in the logo, very few stray from using the pig. This is an example of one that includes a chicken, a popular secondary entree – the dancing is optional.

Sometimes, no visual identity is needed save for a few key elements. City Limits in West Columbia is the perfect example of this. It has a big sign out front that simply says "BBQ". Look a little closer and there's an American flag, a South Carolina flag, and a Texas flag – now you know what they serve. I suppose it helps that pitmaster Robbie Robinson has been nominated for two James Beard awards and the restaurant topped *Southern Living's* Top 25 BBQ Joints in the South Today in 2025.[27]

27. City Limits has earned its reputation through serving great food made the low and slow way. It's worth planning a trip around. https://www.southernliving.com/barbecue-joints-2025-11781538

Bucky's Bar-b-q took their statue in the main dining room to a monumental scale. It is a human-size replica of the pig chef that is represented in their logo. They created an actual mascot that customers can visit. One thing to note, every one of these that I have observed in person is always standing upright on its two hind legs.

Mike & Jeff's BBQ exemplifies the visual inconsistency often found in traditional barbecue joints. While the main sign presents one version of the logo, other signage and ephemera diverge. Rather than detracting from the brand, this inconsistency feels intentional, reinforcing an old-school character and a distinct sense of place.

UPSTATE BARBECUE
BRAND IDENTITIES
Circa 2026

This collection is subdivided by whether or not a pig is included as a part of the identity.

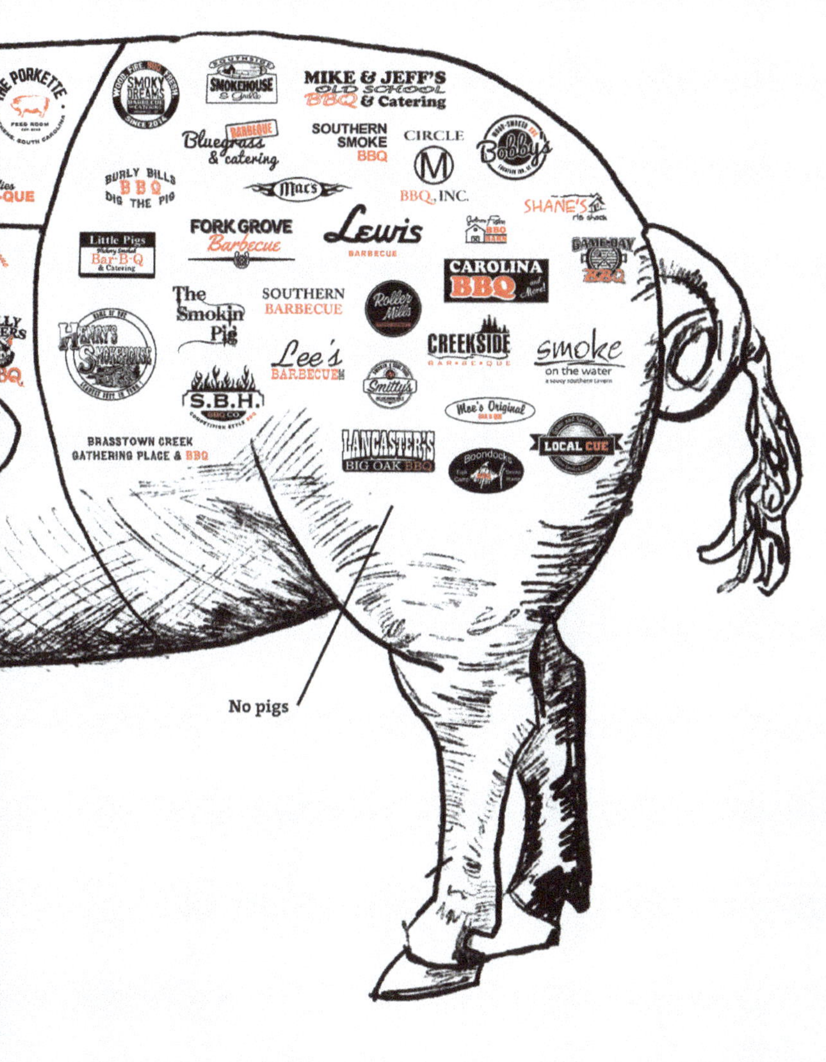

THE PORKETTE
SMOKY DREAMS BARBECUE SINCE 2014
SMOKEHOUSE & Grille
MIKE & JEFF'S OLD SCHOOL BBQ & Catering
Bluegrass BARBECUE & catering
SOUTHERN SMOKE BBQ
CIRCLE M BBQ, INC.
Bobby's
BURLY BILLS BBQ DIG THE PIG
Mac's
SHANE'S rib shack
-QUE
Little Pigs Bar-B-Q & Catering
FORK GROVE Barbecue
Lewis BARBECUE
GAME DAY BBQ
CAROLINA BBQ and More!
The Smokin Pig
SOUTHERN BARBECUE
Roller Mills
HENRY'S SMOKEHOUSE
Lee's BARBECUE
CREEKSIDE BAR-B-QUE
smoke on the water a saucy southern tavern
Smitty's
S.B.H. BBQ CO.
Moe's Original BAR B QUE
LOCAL CUE
BRASSTOWN CREEK GATHERING PLACE & BBQ
LANCASTER'S BIG OAK BBQ
Boondocks
No pigs

THE
REAL
DEAL

TRUTH IN BARBECUE

In my research and conversations, everyone has been pretty gracious when it comes to defining what the cuisine is. There are definitely regional rivalries, and participants will beat their chest over which is the ultimate type of barbecue, but in the end, more often than not, everyone will concede to the fact that if any type of barbecue is done well, it's a great thing to experience.

Wood pile at Rodney Scott's Whole Hog BBQ in Charleston, South Carolina

Jaime Jones, an amateur South Carolinian pitmaster, said it best when I interviewed him:

When I asked him for an example of it being done poorly, he responded:

> *There's people that take shortcuts. I've [seen] people that they'll pass off barbecue as something they throw in the crock pot and cook down for a while or instead of smoking it, they'll just kind of roast it and then add Liquid Smoke into their sauce or something like that. That's not barbecue and to me, it's just cooked meat.*

Essentially, as long as someone makes an attempt at making barbecue the "low and slow" way, they'll earn the respect of the elders. Low and slow is step one. Step two is using real wood. It seems that the die hard barbecue fans will forgive a restaurant for just focusing on shoulders and hams (rather than the whole hog) – heck, the whole Piedmont region of North Carolina does that. But, if they switch from using real wood to propane, that's a deal breaker.

This is so much of an issue that in 1986 South Carolina passed a bill called the "Truth in Barbecue" act. It required that the Department of Agriculture design and print decals "to be displayed wherever barbecue was sold."[28]

28. South Carolina General Assembly. House. *Require the Department of Agriculture to design and print decals which may be displayed wherever barbeque is sold.* HR 3718. 106th sess., introduced in House March, 27th 1986. https://www. scstatehouse.gov/sess106_1985-1986/bills/3718.htm. A printed version of this bill is featured in the next spread.

"**There [are] a lot of people that [say] oh, if it ain't this then it ain't barbecue. I mean, I've been to Texas and had brisket and I'm like, 'Man, that's awesome.' I appreciate good barbecue even like smoked chickens and stuff like that. I mean, to me, that's barbecue too because you're low smoking it, cooking it. I just appreciate anything that's well done that you can tell that they took their time and they did it the right way. I feel like that's important. I'm not one of those that if it ain't this meat and this sauce it ain't really barbecue. No, if it's well done, I appreciate it."

South Carolina General Assembly
106th Session, 1985-1986

Bill 3718

Current Status

Bill Number: 3718
Ratification Number: 491
Act Number: 442
Introducing Body: House
Subject: Require the Department of Agriculture to
                        design and print decals which may be displayed
                        wherever barbeque is sold

View additional legislative information at the LPITS web site.

(Text matches printed bills. Document has been reformatted to meet World Wide Web specifications.)

(A442, R491, H3718)

AN ACT TO REQUIRE THE DEPARTMENT OF AGRICULTURE TO DESIGN AND PRINT DECALS WHICH MAY BE DISPLAYED WHEREVER BARBEQUE IS SOLD AND TO PROVIDE PENALTIES.

Be it enacted by the General Assembly of the State of South Carolina:

Barbeque decals

SECTION 1. The Department of Agriculture shall design and print distinctive decals which may be displayed wherever barbeque is sold. Each decal must state one of the following:

(1) "Barbeque - Whole hog - Cooked with wood".

(2) "Barbeque - Whole hog - Cooked from a heat source other than wood".

(3) "Barbeque - Part of, but not whole hog - Cooked from any source of heat".

(4) "Barbeque - Part of, but not whole hog - Cooked with wood".

Any person who uses a decal which falsely states the type barbeque sold by him is guilty of a misdemeanor and upon conviction must be fined not more than two hundred dollars or imprisoned for not more than thirty days.

Time effective

SECTION 2. This act shall take effect upon approval by the Governor.

According to the bill, the decals should state one of the following:

Displaying the stickers falsely would result in a misdemeanor and a fine. Robert Moss wrote about this bill as well and said that there was a "major shortcoming in the measure: It stated that restaurants may display the decals, but it didn't require them to."[29] Because of this, it fell off the radar and eventually was repealed in 1992.

As far as the wood that is used, it seems to be mainly what is regional. According to Jaime, he uses oak, hickory, and pecan – the same woods commonly used by Rodney Scott, the world-famous South Carolina pitmaster. Jaime explained it this way:

I mean the wood that you use has to be right. I've used wood that was too dry before and it would just burn up. It wouldn't make coals so I was kind of in a panic. And I've played with that a little bit and what I think makes the best smoke because you want good smoke but yet you want good coals to hold temperature for a while. So I use pecan and hickory. They're kind of related so they make about the same kind of smoke… I like the green hickory. I'll throw it in there just because I think it, the green makes more smoke, it's more pungent. But I throw oak in too, just because oak burns well. It makes good coals.

Wood is part of the science of barbecue. It's another variable that takes skill to control, something that is much more difficult than turning on a propane gas line. There are flavors in the smoke that are adjusted in the same way that any seasonings are. Talking to Jaime (and tasting the difference) made it clear to me why there is an adamant following of wood coal enthusiasts, and why they feel there should be transparency on the part of the restaurants as to how they prepare the dish.

I did some digging into finding out more information about the SC Department of Agriculture Truth in Barbecue decal designs. It seems they are lost to history, if they ever were designed in the first place. Either way, I don't think you could find better proof of how seriously South Carolinians are about their barbecue.

BAR·B·Q
THE
MIDLANDS
WORLD'S
BEST
BAR·B·Q
DINING ROOM
OPEN

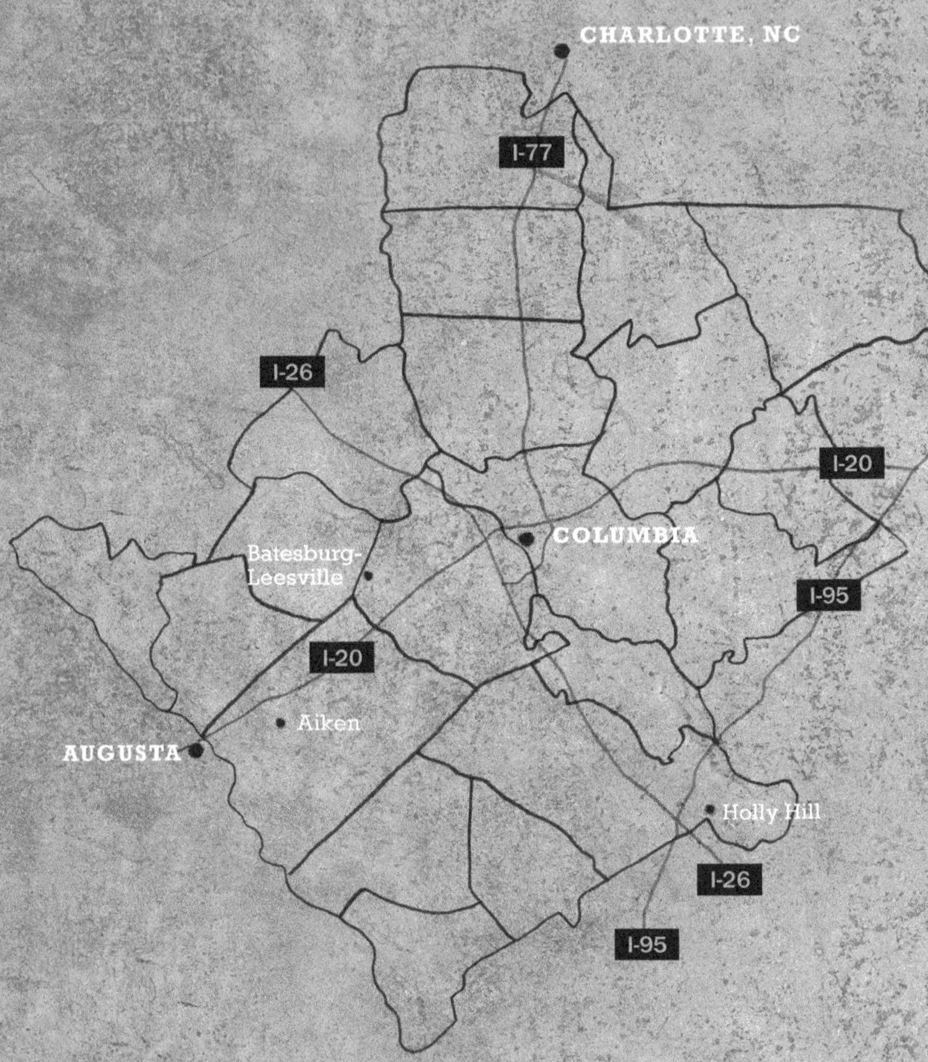

The MIDLANDS REGION of SOUTH CAROLINA

This is home of the capital city of Columbia, and the famed mustard sauce. Politics and barbecue have always gone hand-in-hand. This region exemplifies the relationship as it is the hub for both in South Carolina.

OVERVIEW

Interstates 385 and 26 meet southeast of Greenville combining
to form a blacktop artery down to Columbia, the capital city. This
is the dominant economic area of the Midlands region – 11 counties make up that swath of the state. Aiken County is known for
horses, I know that much. Saluda is named after a popular rafting
river that runs through the region. Mostly, I think of the Midlands
as I learned about the area in middle school. It was called the
sandhills after the sandy dunes that rolled across that part of the
state in a diagonal line that mirrored the coast. Millions of years
ago, it was a coastline. Columbia is sometimes referred to as the
armpit of the state. Imagine the sun and heat you would have on
a beach in the summertime, but take away the sea breeze and
the ocean – that's Columbia.

It's really not all bad though. Columbia reminds me of Tallahas-
see, Florida, where I went to college. It's made up of the state
legislature as well as the other big state school – the University
of South Carolina. A high density of college students and
conservative legislators are indicative of the social opposition

balancing act that exists all over. Where Clemson is agriculturally focused, USC has well-developed fine art and performing arts programs. It focuses on the humanities, and has a prominent international business school. It's an appropriate university to be sitting in the middle of the second-largest metro area. In contrast, Columbia weighs in with its fair share of history that shouldn't be overlooked.

William Tecumseh Sherman's[30] army came through during the Civil War and battered up the state house pretty bad. There are still bronze stars peppering the exterior to show where cannon-balls pummeled the walls. This is the same state house where the confederate battle flag was re-erected in the sixties claiming some loose association to heritage, when it truly was meant to be a stake in the ground supporting social inequality. That flag was permanently removed from the grounds of the state house in 2015 after a brutal massacre at the Emmanuel AME church in Charleston. The fact that its removal was protested reinforced the notion that we have a long way to go as a society when it comes to loving our neighbor.

So, how does barbecue play into all of this? For one, this is the epicenter of the mustard-based sauce that the state is famous for. It is also the home of one of the most infamous chains of barbecue restaurants that has ever existed in the state with a history that mirrors the region's own.

---

30. Union general during the American Civil War. Famously led a scorched earth campaign through the South – capturing Atlanta, and inflicting irreparable damage to the region's infrastucture, inevitably leading to surrender to the North. Although a major influence on the ending of the war, the tactics and execution were (and still are) not seen in a wholly positive light.

→ NOW
ENTERING
FIEFDOM
TERRITORY

SHAKEN
LEGACY
L. Maurice Bessinger, Sr.
Founder
July 14, 1930 - February 22, 2014
PULLED CHICKEN

MAURICE'S PIGGIE PARK

The Midlands is the heart of the state as well as its barbecue. It's a straight shot down I-26 from Greenville where things get a little flatter and a little hotter. It's reportedly where the famed mustard sauce originated,[31] and the Bessinger family that made it popular. Joe Bessinger started a barbecue shop in a little town named Holly Hill between Charleston and Columbia.[32]

31. Robert Moss has a good write up on this phenomenon in his book, *Barbecue Lover's The Carolinas* (pg 110). He says that the sauce "is often attributed to the German influence in what is known as the Dutch Fork, which takes its name from the spot where the Broad and Saluda Rivers meet to form the Congaree and from the number of Germans (or Deutsch) who settled in the area." Apparently Germans didn't only bring mustard to the cuisine, they may have also influenced the vinegar flavors as well as the usage of the shoulder of the hog in the Piedmont regions of North Carolina.
32. Moss, *Barbecue Lover's The Carolinas*, 112

Joe had 11 children, and many of them opened up barbecue restaurants all over the Midlands and Lowlands of the state. There is a lot written about the Bessingers and their barbecue kingdom but the most notorious and emblematic story is the one about Maurice.

Maurice was child number eight and worked at the family's restaurant – he essentially ran the place. Even as a younger sibling, he was in line to take over the Holly Hill staple, but when old Joe died unexpectedly, his older brother, Melvin, ended up claiming the establishment instead. This set off a chain of events for Maurice that included going to college at the Citadel, fighting in the Korean War, and eventually opening his own series of barbecue restaurants. He settled in Columbia after some failed attempts in various cities, and opened up Maurice's BBQ. This grew to be the largest barbecue chain in South Carolina and included sit-down fast-food style restaurants and some drive-in establishments called Maurice's Piggie Park.[33] What really made Maurice a big success is the packaging and marketing of his dad's mustard sauce recipe. Melvin owned the copyright to the original name "Golden Secret," so Maurice renamed his sauce "Southern Gold," and it was sold all over the state in his restaurants and grocery stores.

All of this may seem like a little brother fighting to have his rightful place at the adult table, until you look at what made Maurice Bessinger an infamous character. South Carolina has a storied history of being a hot spot in the fight for civil rights, and Maurice was no stranger to this. He was a very public white supremacist

---

33. The Piggie Park name was used by some of the other Bessinger siblings as they tried to open up more restaurants around the Midlands and Lowcountry. Hence the need for the qualifier, Maurice's, to distinguish it from the family competition. Fertel, *The One True Barbecue*, 156

and refused service to African Americans at his establishments. This caused a 1966 complaint to the FBI from J.W. Mungin, an African American minister, that developed into a civil rights case that made it to the Supreme Court.[34] Needless to say, Maurice lost, but that didn't change his view on equal rights for people of color. In addition to being outspoken from a business perspective, he also was politically driven. He was George Wallace's local campaign manager and ran for South Carolina governor himself in the 1970s under a white supremacist agenda. Piggie Park was South Carolina's most famous barbecue icon. It just wasn't as famous for serving pork as it was for delivering hate speech and racist propaganda.

Main entrance to Maurice's Piggy Park

34. Moss, *Barbecue, The History of an American Institution*, 214

Maurice Bessinger was an outspoken figure for many years, but it wasn't until the year 2000 that he received his comeuppance. The same day that the confederate battle flag was taken down from atop the state house and moved to a not-so-inconspicuous monument honoring the confederate dead on the capitol grounds,[35] he decided to raise the flag at all of his restaurant locations. This set off a chain of events and protests, not only from customers but from grocery stores and other retail businesses where they opted not to sell his famous golden mustard sauce anymore. The NAACP called for a boycott, and national news media pounced on the story. After extended battles in court, Maurice eventually lost all contests. He claimed in his 2004 autobiography that they lost 98% of their sauce business from the decision and it never fully recovered.[36]

Maurice retired in 2010 and passed away in 2014. Since then, Lloyd Bessinger has run the business with his brother, Paul, and their sister, Debbie Bennett. In a *Charlotte Observer* article by Kathleen Purvis, Lloyd said "we want to serve great barbecue and be known for that. Not for politics." The family has made it clear (children and siblings alike) that they do not agree with the message that Maurice's policies sent and want to change that. I suppose only time will tell, but it seems that it is the beginning of a new chapter for Piggie Park, one that is based around a more inclusive message.[37]

All of that context is necessary in understanding why it is important to feature Maurice's original Piggie Park as a case study, and also why my stomach turned when deciding to become a patron of an establishment that has brazenly protested many ideals that I

35. Fertel, *The One True Barbecue*, 159
36. Moss, *Barbecue Lover's The Carolinas*, 113
37. Purvis, *Can a S.C. Barbecue Family Rise above Their Father's History of Racism?*

strongly believe in. When I drove into West Columbia on a humid day in July, the gigantic Piggie Park sign literally took my breath away. It was a symbol as exaggerated as the former owner, daring me to turn back.

The sign could've been located on the Las Vegas strip. I was there during the afternoon, so I'm not sure if there were lights to match, but it certainly could have fared well alongside the old Dunes or Golden Nugget casino marquees. They both had similar goals in luring people in off the street – granted, Columbia doesn't have as much competition as Vegas. There is a large anthropomorphic pig, standing atop the sign. He has on a baseball cap and a t-shirt that reads "Little Joe," an obvious nod to the patriarch of the Bessinger clan and to the history of the family's connection with barbecue. Underneath Little Joe is the word "Bar-B-Q" in a slab-serif typeface that invokes the Wild West nature of the original owner. This may explain the wry smile on Little Joe as he gives passing motorists the side eye.

Vintage Las Vegas postcards, courtesy of the author

LITTLE JOE
BAR-B-Q
Since 1959
Piggie Park
GO   GAMECOCKS
TAILGATE WITH US
RIBS   CHICKEN
WINGS BRISKET

I kept driving, watching the tendril of smoke creep up into the sky as the sign grew larger on the horizon. Beside it, a giant American flag came into view—one of the largest I've ever seen. I remembered an image of Maurice standing under the sign with the confederate flag waving in the background – this must be the same place. In the photo, the sky loomed large overhead. In driving up, I saw what was not shown in the frame: an industrial highway converging into a five road intersection with a tangle of power lines, stop lights, and traffic interrupting the view. The restaurant was situated on a piece of land that jutted out into the mess (see photo on following page). There was another sign on the traffic light side of the building that was just a giant Q.

In this area of the country, just the letter can signify barbecue. The South Carolina Barbecue Association can attest, as its logo is just that – one large Q.

There was the restaurant itself complete with a dining room and drive through. The parking lot was covered in three rows of long sheds. They looked like long carports and floated over the parking spaces, remnants of the restaurant's drive-in history. If you want to eat in the car now, you have to order at the drive through window, or go inside and bring it back out. In a way, the metal structures help the restaurant sit in a nostalgic purgatory – not quite old enough to hearken the "good old days" but not new enough to still have its sheen. The corporate offices and smokehouse used to exist on the other side of the parking lot, but they unfortunately burned down in 2024. The restaurant

MAURICE'S
Piggie Park
ONLY
MAURICE'S
Piggie Park

BAR·B·Q
LITTLE JOE
WORLD'S
BEST
BAR-B-Q
RESTAURANT
PARKING

closed for a bit of time to recover, but now they're running again with a makeshift smokehouse taking up a portion of the parking lot. There are still piles of wood, and a big chimney with a trail of smoke you can see from a distance. Those wood piles are probably one of the main reasons Maurice's still has credibility in the state's barbecue ranks. Using real wood and not charcoal or gas to smoke a pig is the only real way to make South Carolina barbecue, after all.

Piggie Park wasn't dirty, but it felt past its prime. I'm not sure if it was because it had rained a good bit that day, or if my own biases were clouding my perception of the place (I really tried to be conscious of this), but it felt a bit tired. I couldn't help but think it was a series of unplanned additions that kept getting added as the restaurant grew. The drive through cut right across the main entrance, forcing customers that wanted to go inside to potentially weave in between cars to reach the front steps. The thing is, it wouldn't surprise me if it had always been this way. There was a sense of impermanence about the whole structure even though it has been in that same spot for around 70 years.

I wanted to have the experience of eating in the parking area, so I ordered using the drive through. The menu signage reminded me of many fast food establishments before flat panel displays took over with their animated menus. The menu started with a list of sandwiches and moved on to a "build your own plate" section. Both featured pork, chicken, ribs and brisket. There were other items like hamburgers and smoked turkey offered perhaps for those in the family who weren't fans of the traditional spread. The sides offered were the standard mac and cheese, potato salad, fried okra, and baked beans. Hash and rice was also on the menu – it's a South Carolina specialty. Hash has been described as a meat soup, or gravy. Think of the ingredients of sausage but puréed. I absolutely adore hash.

I ordered a barbecue pulled pork plate with fried okra and hash and rice for the sides – no messing around here. Once I had retrieved my food from the drive through window, I found a parking spot in one of the carport shed spaces in front of the main entrance and proceeded to eat my lunch. The barbecue was fine, but it was drowned in so much of the mustard sauce that you couldn't taste the pork. I'm not a barbecue judge, or food writer for that matter, but I will say the barbecue was good. The sauce was super tangy and sweet. The hash and rice was fine, and the okra was great. I'm a huge fan of fried okra, and as long as it's

Hash and rice, fried okra, and barbecue with a mustardy tinge

A wall of barbecue sauce

not burnt it's generally hard to mess up. The color palette of the plate was overwhelmingly brown with a little green and a tinge of yellow. If you had amnesia and found yourself with a plate of barbecue in your lap that was this color, it would be a huge clue that you were in the South Carolina Midlands. It's a pretty typical visual for this cuisine. The styrofoam plate that is divided into three sections is a barbecue staple. Using the plastic utensils to fork the food into my mouth while not dripping the yellow sauce on my pants made me feel like I was following in the footsteps of the thousands who've come before me, all while parked under the sign featuring a giant version of Little Joe.

After I finished my plate, I decided to go inside and check out the restaurant. I looked both ways, opened the front door, and was met with a wall of barbecue sauce. There were five different flavors, all packaged in plastic bottles with glossy labels. Every bottle featured the white-haired Maurice himself residing over the trademarked "Southern Gold" moniker set in a slab serif. This bottle at one time had a confederate flag featured as a part of the layout, adding to the list of reasons the grocery store chains in the state pulled it from their shelves. Now, the flag has been replaced with declarations of the establishment's presence on social media, driving a hard stake in the ground that it is indeed part of the 21st century and is here to stay.

I bought a bottle of the original mustard sauce as well as a drink so I could get a good look at the dining room. There were a few customers eating lunch, but the whole space probably could hold 150 people. It was dark. Light was flowing in from the back wall that faced the street, but those were the only windows in the

place. As I filled a styrofoam cup with soda from a fountain, I noticed a human-sized cut out sign of Little Joe on the wall beside the register where I placed my order. There was a floor graphic stating where one should stand for the photo op. This reinforced a thought I'd had in the back of my mind since I'd parked: Piggie Park is a tourist attraction. In the same way people may want their picture taken with Mickey Mouse, Little Joe was an attempt at kindling some kind of nostalgic empathy with the place. Surrounding the mascot were images from the restaurants past, many featuring Maurice himself.

I'd been told that there was once a stack of white supremacist pamphlets by the front door – a kind of welcome that said more about the man than the menu. I'm relieved to say there's nothing like that now. The tone of the place has quieted into something more neutral, as if it's trying to hold on to the name while letting the rest fade with time.

If the current owners keep moving in this direction, Piggie Park could stand again as a landmark of Columbia's barbecue history – its legacy tied to the food Joe Bessinger helped bring into South Carolina's culture rather than the divisions his son became known for. In that light, Maurice's story becomes just one chapter in a longer, more complicated family history – one that mirrors both the best and hardest parts of the state's past.

Inside, I looked up at the portrait of Maurice in his white suit, smiling back at me from the wall. He feels less like a founder now and more like a relic – a symbol that lingers because no one quite knows what to do with it.

The mustard sauce packaging then and now. Social media icons have replaced the Confederate imagery. The image on the left was taken by Jason Perlow in 2008. The image on the right is my own from 2020.

Out in the parking lot, I sat in my car for a while, thinking about Lolis Eric Elie's words in *Smokestack Lightning*. He quoted Jane and Michael Stern, who once wrote, "Dining at Maurice Bessinger's is a stirring experience… the kind of uniquely American meal to which we would eagerly take visitors from another country if we wanted to show the spunk, character, and quality of American gastronomy."[38] Elie envied their enthusiasm but wasn't as moved. I knew what he meant.

The place feels caught between remembering and rewriting – between the story it tells and the one it leaves unsaid. What remains is a tension you can't quite shake, like smoke that's settled deep into the walls – faint but still there.

38. This book was recommended to me by Rien Fertel. Probably the first great book telling the stories of barbecue and pitmasters around the South. Elie, *Smokestack Lightning*, 158

SIDE EYE
LITTLE JOE

ALL
SPELLINGS
WELCOME
GOLF WITH YOUR FRIENDS
PLATE
All Plates Served w
Regular Sandwich Plat
Hog Sandwich Plate
Chopped Pork Plate
Smoked Chicken Plate
Combination
Pork, Chicken
Choice of any 2
Choice of any 3
Henry's Ribs ½ Rack
Henry's Ribs Full Rack
Hash and Rice
SIDE
Beans
Slaw
Potato Salad
Green Beans
Sweet Potato Casserc
Macaroni and Cheese
French Fries
Hash and Rice
Brunswick Stew
Rice
Peach Cobbler
Chips (Plain or BBQ)
Henry's Smokehouse
LEN JACOBS
Dog Bones
ServSafe
CERTIFICATION

BARBECUE, BAR-B-QUE, AND BBQ

As I searched, ate, observed, and dissected barbecue across the state, one detail kept demanding a closer look: how to properly spell the word *barbecue*. Earlier, I mentioned that the culinary origins of the practice can be traced to the Taino Indians; here, I turn to the word itself, following its evolution from *baribicu*, to the Spanish *barbacoa*, and finally to the modern *barbecue* – now with a c.

When you start looking at the vernacular use of the word, it seems to change from place to place. And I don't mean region to region – I mean restaurant to restaurant to painted sign to print advertisement. There are a slew of different ways to spell it and pretty much all of them are a-okay. I'll attempt to break down where they came from.

95

Barbecue is favored by the dictionary and also the state of North Carolina. This is appropriate, considering the state's self-proclaimed title as the capital of barbecue. The North Carolina Barbecue Association's website spells it with a c, and that is what they stand behind as an organization. On the other hand, South Carolina spells it with a *q* – as in *barbeque.*

According to Jack Hitt on the Southern Foodways Alliance website:

> *Like everything in South Carolina, we cook barbeque cantankerously. We smoke our meat with hundreds of opinions and often with a sense of injured pride. Otherwise, it's just different in South Carolina – all the way down to the way we spell it, more often with the garish and trashy "q" rather than the upwardly mobile and buttoned-down "c."* [39]

More garish and trashy is a fitting hyperbole. There is a hint of sarcasm in that statement, and I think it's a perfect analogy between the differences in the two states. Some get the Carolinas confused – this statement should help alleviate that confusion.

The other popular spellings I found in my exploration of South Carolina restaurants were bar-b-que, bar-b-q, and the concise BBQ. From what I can gather, these other spellings came about when restaurants started advertising their wares in the 1920s. According to Robert Moss, the shortened bar-b-q "saved proprietors three expensive letters."[40] This carried on even more so after World War II when the non-acronym BBQ came into play.

39. Hitt, *South Carolina BBQ*
40. Moss, *How Do You Spell Barbecue?*

ANNOUNCING

The Re-Opening Of

BOYD'S

PIT

BARBECUE

UNDER THE ORIGINAL
OWNERSHIP AND MANAGEMENT

W. G. BOYD

We Will Be Happy To See and Serve Our Old Customers
Who Enjoyed Our Tasty Variety of
Good Things To Eat!

OLD FASHIONED PIT BARBECUE
LAMB and PORK and BRUNSWICK STEW
Curb Service ● Dining Room ● Home Package

AUGUSTA STREET ——Just Beyond City Limits

BAR-B-QUE NIGHT 4 pm to 8:30 pm
BBQ PORK, BBQ RIBS OF BEEF
BBQ CHICKEN, BBQ STRIPS W/RICE

Also Baked Ham Fish & Chicken 7 Vegetables
24 Salads And Complimentary Seconds

BRING THIS WITH YOU AND PAY

This Coupon Valid For
$2.60 Dinner On
9-20-77   ONLY **$2.60**

FOREST ACRES
2120 BELTLINE BLVD.
Phone 782-6367

Sir George's ROYAL BUFFET

Now thru the
4TH

Old Fashioned Hickory Flavored

BAR·B·Q

Spare Ribs   Chopped Bar-B-Q
Bar-B-Q Hash   Bar-B-Q Chicken
Bar-B-Q Beans   Cole Slaw

Sandwiches   Bar-B-Q Plates

By-The-Pound

**OPEN 8 A.M., JULY 4
PLACE YOUR ORDER EARLY**

PIT BARBECUE

We are pleading with the people who
enjoy old fashioned pit cooked barbecue
to call by our place, to convince you what
we have to offer. We are running special
prices on hams, shoulders and loins
weighing from 5 to 10 pounds at 80c per
pound, to be delivered to your home or
business address. Let us solve your table
problems.

Fonville's Barbecue Pit
Opposite Southern Depot. Phone 1663

*Various spellings of "barbecue" in
newspaper advertisements from
the early to mid-twentieth century*

*Clockwise from top left: Boyd's Pit Barbe-
cue, The Greenville News, July 18, 1938;
Bar B Q Pit, The State, July 30, 1972;
Fonville's Barbecue Pit, The Greenville
News, September 5, 1929; Sir George's
Royal Buffet, The State, September 20,
1977. All images courtesy of the author.*

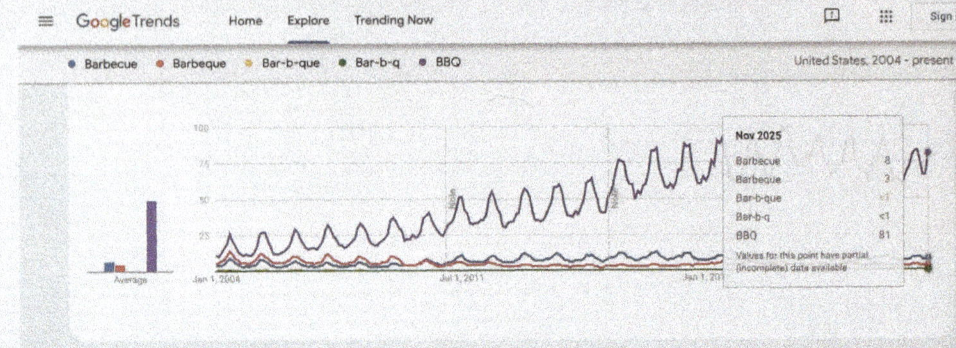

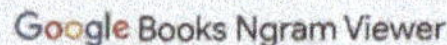

Google Books Ngram Viewer

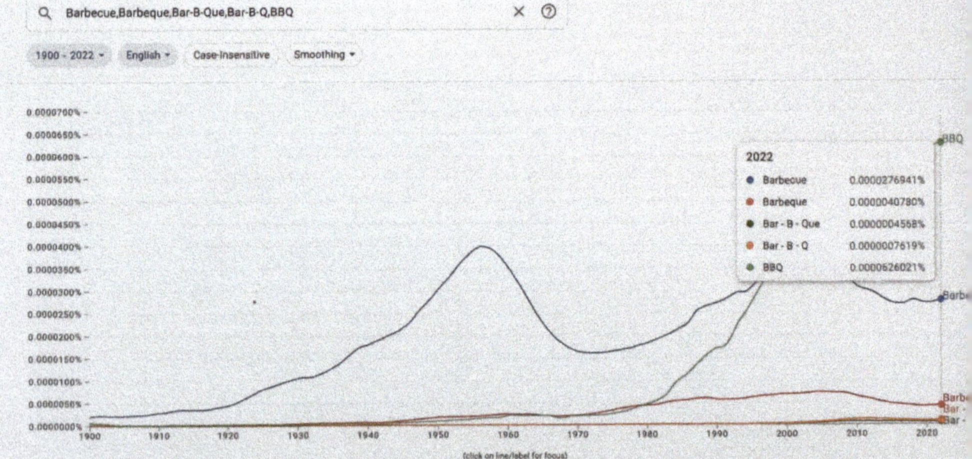

BBQ, BAR-B-QUE & BARBECUE TRENDS

The Google Trends graph on the top shows the most popular search term from the collection of words entered. The Ngram Viewer looks at the most common of the terms used in books.

If a proprietor was charged by the letter to run his ads in the local paper, it makes sense this three-letter version stuck around.

The South Carolina Barbeque Association's logo offers the most abbreviated version I've encountered, with the letter Q dominating the hierarchy. It's reflected in speech in this part of the country where the phrase "we're going to get some Q" needs no explanation.

I searched using Google's Ngram viewer[41] – which searches through books in Google's extensive online database – for the various ways to spell the word. "BBQ" started gaining in traction in the 1980s and is decidedly in the lead now. This aligns with a typical Google web search, the abbreviated BBQ reigns supreme by a large margin when looking at the national interest. In South Carolina, it follows the same trend line. Funny enough though, South Carolina's *q* variant is not as common of a search when compared to the *c* version. I suppose the SCBA needs to push that agenda a bit harder.

41. This is a free tool that can be accessed at the website: https://books.google.com/ngrams

I took a look at my own database of SC restaurants and did a quick count of the uses in this region. The preferred spelling of the barbeque association is third on the list. The second is the official dictionary spelling (barbecue with a *c*) and the first shares the same tastes of the internet public – BBQ. I guess space in ads is still a consideration. In reality, I think it has more to do with it becoming an accepted variation of the word.

THE
PEE DEE

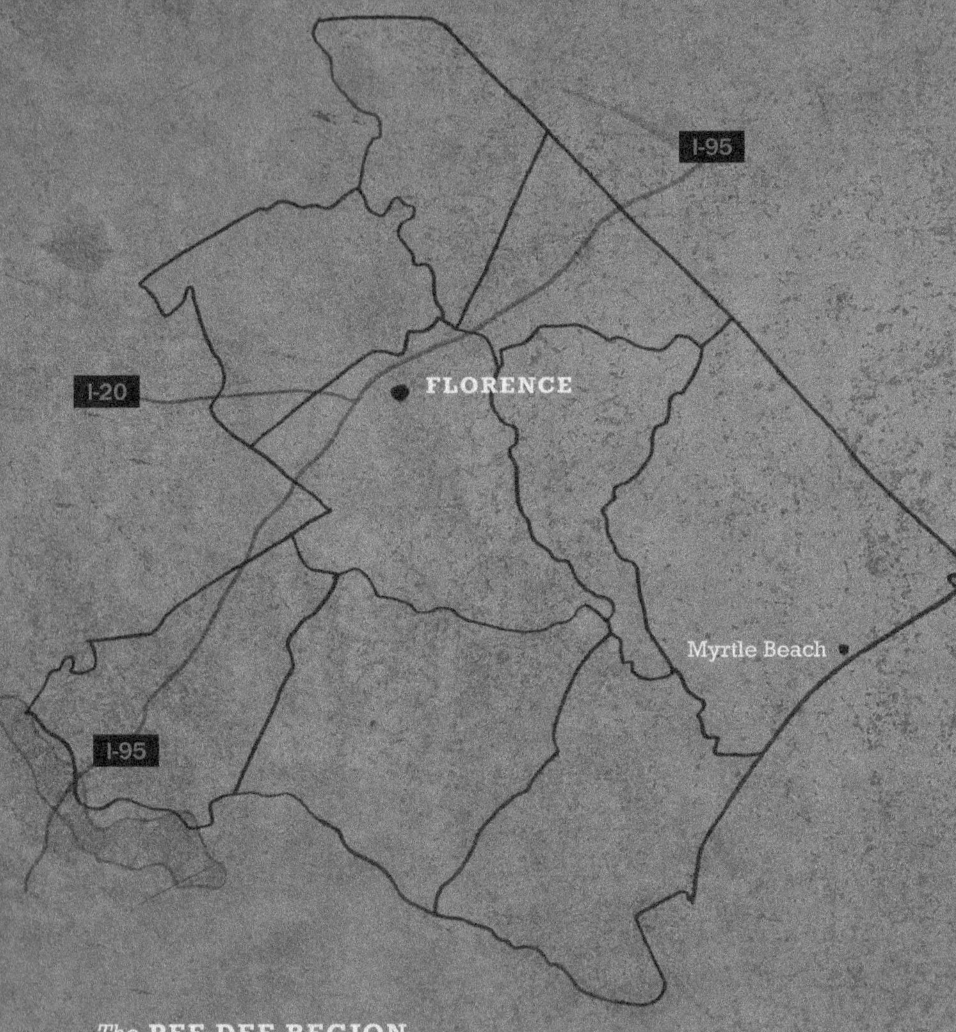

The **PEE DEE REGION** of **SOUTH CAROLINA**

The Pee Dee region shares a similar barbecue style to Eastern North Carolina with the vinegar and pepper sauce and whole-hog cooking. There are few restaurants in this very rural part of the state – but they're all known to serve some of the best barbecue.

OVERVIEW

The names of the other three regions featured in this book have nothing on the Pee Dee. It takes its name from the Pee Dee Native American tribe and the river that runs from North Carolina to the South Carolina coast. The region is among the most widely recognized areas of the state, anchored by the spring breaker paradise of Myrtle Beach.

Any time I meet people from Michigan and they find out where I'm from, they always reference this Grand Strand of beach tourism at its finest. I've been to Myrtle Beach once. I feel like I've got it – I don't need to go back.

The Pee Dee is also home to the strange off-color roadside landmark on I-95 called South of the Border. Long familiar to travelers heading south toward the coast, the attraction is perhaps best summarized by its water tower topped with an oversized sombrero, – and that's all I'm going to say about that.

Florence is the largest city in the Pee Dee, edging out Myrtle Beach by only a few hundred residents, yet it ranks just eleventh statewide.[42] That statistic underscores the region's rural character, something that becomes immediately apparent when driving through its wide expanses of farmland. The landscape feels unhurried – beautiful in a way that suggests another time.

The Pee Dee is one of the most agriculturally productive regions in South Carolina, situated along a broad crescent of fertile topsoil that stretches across much of the South. Cotton once dominated the local economy (there is even a museum devoted to the crop), with tobacco also playing a major role. This area lies squarely within the Southern cotton belt and is often referred to as the Black Belt – a historically rooted term that reflects both the region's dark, fertile soil and its predominantly African American population. A comparison of census maps from the Civil War era to today reveals how little has changed in terms of population patterns and racial inequality.[43]

In terms of barbecue, the Pee Dee region functions largely as a southern extension of eastern North Carolina, favoring smoking whole hogs paired with a vinegar-and-pepper sauce. In recent years, pitmaster Elliott Moss returned to his hometown of Florence after time in Asheville, North Carolina, opening Elliott's BBQ Lounge – a restaurant and brewery that brings a contemporary edge to the region's barbecue landscape. This modern approach stands in contrast to Scott's Bar-B-Que in Hemingway, a quintessential roadside stand that has earned national recognition as one of the country's great whole-hog barbecue joints.

42. South Carolina Demographics, "Cities by Population," accessed December 13, 2025, https://www.southcarolina-demographics. com/cities_by_population

43. This information was gathered from census.gov and historical census maps – comparing 2019 and 1860 census data.

EASTERN SC
HERITAGE REGION

North Carolina
South Carolina
Scott's Bar-B-Que
Vinegar & pepper
Tomato sauce added
Ketchup based
Mustard based
Copyright © AmazingRibs.com

"We put a
love into w

→ GAS IS FOR
CARS
NOT FOR
COOKING
BBQ
-R. SCOTT

SCOTT'S BAR-B-QUE

First impressions are hard to shake.[44]

My first pilgrimage to Scott's was an adventure – one of those trips that settles into memory with the smell of smoke and the thrill of discovery. I've been back since, and much has changed. But the story of that first visit is still worth telling.

I had initially planned to make the trek to the lower part of the state alone, but at the last minute my wife, Jess, and our friend Brigetta

44. My visit to Scott's was especially impactful, so this case study is treated a bit differently than the others.

wanted to join me. They'd heard me talking (ad nauseam) about this particular barbecue destination and wanted to see what all the fuss was about. It was summer, and was the first clear day in a little while. The whole state had been soaked in rain from the previous week, so this was a welcome reprieve from being cooped up indoors. Any excuse for a road trip, right?

The trip each way was around three and a half hours, and we had a roadside view of most of the state's regions in a single day. Scott's Bar-B-Que sits in a small hamlet named Hemingway in the Pee Dee. Without GPS, I imagine it would be near impossible to find. We drove down past Columbia on the interstate and exited the highway with almost two hours to go. That's when I finally understood just how far out-of-the-way this place really was. Long, flat stretches of road gave way to farmland and small houses, and the the remoteness made it feel like a pilgrimage, not just a drive.

It was humid. The kind of humid that caused blurry black mirages to appear on the horizon. We would take a turn here

Opposite: An hour and a half out of the way from anywhere

and there only to be on another road that looked the same. The closer we got, the more we noticed that the fields alongside us had large pools of standing water. Then we started noticing flooded houses. And finally, the mirages in the road started to forgo being illusions and we began driving through water that was streaming from one side of the road to the other like a wide shallow creek. You could make out the lines in the road, but they started to get harder to see and the water patches more frequent as we moved deeper into the country. At one point, we had to turn around when we saw a large pickup truck in front of us driving through water that almost covered the wheels. We were starting to get nervous. Jess was worried we would get stuck. I was too. But what overtook that fear was the possibility that Scott's may not be open due to all of the rain. I imagined it falling into the same fate of these flooded houses that we had been driving by. After about 45 minutes of turning down roads and turning back around due to all of the water, we finally found ourselves on Hemingway highway.

We drove straight for a short while, not passing much of anything except for a few churches and a gorgeously dilapidated ruin of an elementary school. Up ahead, I saw a structure with a baby blue metal roof out beside the trees. As we got closer, it grew larger and turned into a small shack with a front porch and an a-frame roof line. We made it, and there was no standing water in sight. After a quick few minutes of driving around trying to find parking – there's no real parking lot here, you kind of just park on the side of the road – we squeezed in between a pickup truck and a Camaro. We got out of the car and started walking to the front

The "gold at the end of the rainbow" moment of our drive

Barbecue can
of those
PIT
SCOTT

be one
destination places.
—Jaime Jones

of the shop. There was a line of people streaming out of the front door, over the porch, and into the parking area. It was probably ten to twelve people deep from the door to where we ended up standing. This was expected from one of the most well-known barbecue establishments in the state.

Roosevelt Scott (Rosie for short) bought the small variety store in the early 1970s. They sold everyday items and dry goods you may find at a gas station, had a small truck repair shop,[45] and sold whole hog barbecue on some weekends. Over time, word spread and the barbecue became the name of the game. It became the only business, but you can still find watermelons on the front porch and Red Rock strawberry sodas in the fridge.[46] Rosie ran the pits, cooking pork the best way he knew how – whole hogs over a pit of low heat coals for about twelve hours. Low and slow. The skin is side up so the fat can flavor the meat as gravity pulls it down into the embers. That is mixed with the smoke from the wood coals – procured from pecan and oak trees. Near the end of the cooking time, the hogs get flipped and a vinegar pepper sauce is mopped – literally with a mop you may find in cleaning supply closets – into the animal's cavity and simmers for about 20 to 30 minutes before it is taken off. The meat is then pulled out of the pig – the inedible bits thrown away – the light and dark meats mixed together and then served straight to a hungry customer. This technique is similar to the classic technique that is practiced in Eastern North Carolina. The difference is that the Pee Dee region has spicier sauce, and no sauce in the area is as spicy as Scott's.

45. Robert Moss informed me of this in a conversation that I had with him during my research. He said "they would fix trucks and they had a general store, but then started cooking hogs on the weekends to sell at the store. And then that became bigger and bigger, and so they got rid of the garage and turned it into a pit room."

46. Strawberry soda is the drink of choice to pair with barbecue in the Pee Dee region.

It took a while for Scott's to get noticed by the world outside of Hemingway. One can see why after our long, back-road laden, water-impeded drive down there. When they did start attracting foodies and barbecue aficionados, Rosie had long turned over the pitmaster hat to his son Rodney. Rodney had smoked his first hog at age 11 and took over the cooking at 17. He was probably in his late twenties or early thirties by the time Scott's started being written about, and at that point he really knew how to smoke a hog. Rien Fertel describes him in his book *The One True Barbecue* as follows:

> If cooking whole hogs was an Olympic sport – and there is no reason it shouldn't be – Rodney Scott would be our gold medalist. In tiny Hemingway he stands as a barbecue giant. Rodney has the larger-than-life aura of a man who could be famous for doing something other than cooking hogs, combined with the modest attitude of a guy with whom you'd actually like to eat barbecue.[47]

Rodney has since grown to superstardom in the world of barbecue. He has won a James Beard award for Best Chef in the Southeast, only the second pitmaster to have ever received one.[48] He started his own restaurant in Charleston and moved down there. The new place now has branches in Atlanta, Nashville, and a couple in the Birmingham area. It's still whole-hog barbecue, but this time with a full menu and merch for days.

As we were standing in line, I wandered around a little to get a better look at our surroundings. There wasn't much. Across the street was a gated-off empty lot that looked like it may store

47. Fertel, *The One True Barbecue*, 178
48. The first one was given to Aaron Franklin of Franklin Barbecue in Austin, TX.

NO DRUGS OR
LOAFERS
ALLOWED

VOTE Ivori L.
Henryhand
WILLIAMSBURG COUNTY
CORONER
Vision ~ Commitment ~ Compassion

truck trailers, but was pretty much empty at the time. There was a small shelter with three or four picnic tables. I'm not sure how you would access it since the gate was closed and locked. Around the back of the store I saw some stacks of wood and some smoke, but I couldn't quite get back far enough to see anything more. As the line crept its way up to the porch of the building, there were piles of watermelons along the way. Above the watermelons was a sign that read:

"NO DRUGS OR LOAFERS ALLOWED"

At first, I thought "loafer" was referring to the sockless shoes you find all over a town like Charleston, and associating drugs with them made me laugh. I imagined a person wearing a seersucker suit standing in line smoking a joint and wearing loafers, and then a couple of huge pitmasters coming out to ask them to leave. Then I realized that it probably was referring to loitering rather than fashion choices – so much for that fantasy. I also realized very quickly that this sign was in no way decorative as it would be in many a chain restaurant to indicate its folksiness. This was the real deal. There were more signs to come, and they weren't kidding with their messaging. One of the big things that changed in Rodney's new restaurant in Charleston was the fact that he's serving alcohol. That's not something that's done here. They're serious about keeping things civil.

There were a variety of license plates attached to the cars that lined the side of the road – the majority of the clientele were not from around Hemingway. I heard one woman mention that they were from Jacksonville, Florida. I was stunned that someone would make a four-and-a-half hour drive for barbecue and surmised that they must be up here to go to the beach.

This sign caused me to daydream about seersucker suits.

Then I thought of us, and how long we had driven. I guess it isn't that far-fetched after all. This place draws people from all over. There was a gentleman behind me in line (I didn't catch his name) who was from Austin, Texas. He was a marketing professional who worked for a restaurant group that specializes in barbecue restaurant concepts. He and his family were on their way to Myrtle Beach, and he "drug them an hour out of the way" so he could see the place that "everyone keeps talking about." This must've been one of those research trips on how to recreate the authenticity of the old restaurants in the new ones. This guy was genuinely excited to be here – he said he had been trying to visit Scott's for years.

There was a mix of race and ethnicity in the visitors. The Pee Dee region is predominantly African American,[49] and the Scotts themselves were Black, along with most of the employees that I could see. This situation was a stark contrast from my experience at Maurice's in Columbia – the crowd and employees there had majority white complexions when I visited. I'm not sure if this is location based or due to the history of racial injustice connected to the Midlands chain – either way, this small shack on the side of the road was a relief. People were united behind great cuisine. No one seemed to care where you were from or what you looked like. I could be reading a heck of a lot into it, but it felt significant.

When we arrived at the door, waiting our turn to go inside the store, Rosie was sitting in an old church pew turned porch bench presiding over all who entered. He was there with a couple of friends who talked a lot more than he did, but they may have

49. Counties in the Pee Dee region of the state range from 40-73% Black or African American according to 2019 census data on the census.gov website.

Top image: Roosevelt "Rosie" Scott, seated at left, with others at Scott's Bar-B-Que
Bottom image: the line at Scott's Bar-B-Que

Top left image: Image by peedeefolks.net (no credit given). Posted in 2013
Top right image: Image by fedguides.com (no credit given). Taken between 2015-18 after the new pithouse was built
Middle image: Signs in Summer of 2020
Bottom image: Signs in Spring of 2025 – note the memorial to Rosie Scott

been employees too. They all wore matching work shirts with their names embroidered on the chest. They looked like they could have been left over from the building's previous life as a repair shop. It wouldn't have surprised me. The building we were standing in front of carried layers upon layers of reinvention. If this had been in Greenville, Columbia, or Charleston, it would have most likely been torn down or at least renovated with each new chapter. But here, when change came, it simply happened. Remnants stayed, additions were tacked on, and the result was an aesthetic that felt unpolished, but deeply honest – one you couldn't fabricate if you tried.

Rosie has since passed, but he hasn't been forgotten. A large sign affixed to the front of the building honors his memory and enduring importance to this place. It's not just a tribute – it's part of a larger collection of lived-in objects that trace the story of Scott's. These aren't just remnants. They're artifacts. A kind of living museum that documents the people and events that shaped the business.

That memorial is now the latest layer on the most iconic of those artifacts: the sign out front. In years past, it read:

SCOTTS VARIETY

in movable plastic type with some missing letters. Beside it was a hammered-up piece of painted plywood that read:

SCOTT'S PIT COOK B.B.Q.

and a phone number. There was the ubiquitous pig laying on top of what looked like a cube with transparent sides – meant to represent the pit. It was clear so it would showcase the wood and flames inside. Of course, there are no flames in a real pit, only coals. But the coals are born from fire, and the hogs are smoked with wood. That matters. The sign was visually descriptive, albeit literal and slightly inaccurate, but it communicated exactly what it needed to.

In a newer phase, this multi-sign montage was replaced with one that focused entirely on barbecue. I'm not sure if this happened when Rodney moved to Charleston, or if it was just an evolutionary update that occurred along the same lines of changes in the past. Nevertheless, this is the foundation of what is there today. The old letters and plywood were removed and a new piece of plywood was erected. It is entirely hand painted in red and black with the words:

PIT COOK SCOTT's B.B.Q.

emblazoned across the front. In addition to the letters, there is an animal painted in all black with a white collar and a phone number across its belly. The figure is unique in that it seems to be a hybrid between a pig and a dog. I may be reading too much into what may just be a unskilled painter's attempt at a pig, but there are some things about the sign that say otherwise. I'm not sure I've ever seen a pig with a collar. The ears and shape of its snout also seem to be that of a pit bull, implying a play on words with the word "pit" that sits beside the animal's head.

The new sign

This is a much different take than the popular anthropomorphic, or just plain butcher diagram, pigs you see in other restaurants across the state. Another indication that the haphazard painting technique may have been intentional is all the droplets of paint coming from the words and the animal. At first glance, I assumed it was painted in a vertical fashion, causing the paint to drip down the sign. But after looking more closely, I saw that the drops were painted on, resembling iconographic water droplets. There is something menacing about the sign. It may be the red, black, and white color scheme, or the imposing pit bull hog with what seems to be only three legs guarding the front door. One thing it makes clear is what is made and sold at this establishment, and I imagine that is the goal of the new sign in the first place.

We made it through the front door and found ourselves in a much shorter line of two groups of people counting the three of us. There were a few tables and chairs stacked in the corner and refrigerators with a variety of Pepsi products along the back wall, and cases of Red Rock strawberry soda on the floor. To the left of the door as we walked in, a bar sat unused. It looked like it normally would serve lemonade or other beverages, but I wondered if it was more a remnant of the past. The action was happening to the right of the door. Along the far right wall was a window where there were two women hustling about – one was taking food orders, and the other was taking cash. Above the window was the menu, a no-nonsense chalkboard neatly inscribed with the current offerings. The left column included whole hog options, but also included entire chickens and turkeys. Scott's does a lot of business when it comes to serving large groups of people. In the the right column were the single entree sized options. Essentially, you could choose between a few barbecue (pork) options and chicken. There were three sides: baked beans, coleslaw, and potato salad. The holy trinity. And that's about all there was to it.

To the right of the menu was a large piece of fluorescent green poster board that read:

"Please Read"
You must have on
"shirt", "shoes",
and "no drop down
pants" or you will
be asked to leave!
Thank You
The Manager

Scott's   BBQ   Menu
Whole Hog $600.00   BBQ   lB $12.00
1/2 Hog $300.00   BBQ Sandwich $6.00
1/4 Hog $150.00   Chicken Sandwich $5.00
Whole Chicken $10.00   BBQ Plate with sides $9.
Turkey $50.00   Chicken Plate with sides $8.
To Cook your hog $135.00   BBQ Ribs lB $12
Gallon of Sauce $25.00   Sides Bo
                            $1.00 M
NO DEBIT
SORRY
WE DO NOT
ACCEPT
CREDIT CARDS
Place Order Here
Pay
FREEDOM FESTIVAL
NEWMAN
TRACTOR PULLS

"Please Read"
You must have on
"Shirt", "Shoes",
and "no drop down
Pants" Or you will
be asked to leave!
PLEASE HAVE
MONEY READY
CASHIER
Thank You
The Manager
CAUCE
25.00
12.50
7.00
3.00
SNICKERS
Variety Pack
SORRY
WE DO NOT
ACCEPT
CREDIT CARDS
TAS
One

This is obviously a play on the "no shirts, no shoes, no service" sign that one may see in retail establishments, but the drop down pants line indicates a recurring problem that the sign is attempting to rectify. I have no doubt in my mind that they mean what they say.

The last sign worth mentioning hangs on the wall to the right of the poster board, above the door to the area behind the window. It's printed in block letterforms:

CREDIT IS "DEAD"
FUNERAL "NOON" SAT.
PLACE COUNTY JAIL
BURIAL IN "HELL"
REV. "DEVIL" IN CHARGE
- THE MANAGER

I had read about this particular sign before coming here – so we were prepared. It's less a message than a performance: a sermon in all caps, warning that only cash buys blessings here. It also seems to be the only attempt at humor in the signage – at least, I think it's meant to be funny. What I do know is they don't take credit cards, so you'd better come ready. Cash-only businesses are increasingly rare, but they still show up in places like this – family-run, rooted, a little resistant. In recent years, Venmo and Square have made quiet appearances, but avoiding credit card fees remains the priority. And really, who can blame them?

We finally made our way up to the window. Two orders of chicken and one barbecue plate with potato salad and baked beans, one pint of sauce, and one small sandwich bag of pig skins.
The woman who took our order was older and sharp as a tack.

She was Ella Scott, Rosie's wife, and – if I had to guess – the one credited as "The Manager" in the sign hanging inside. She moved with calm precision, pulling pork, scooping sides, stacking plates, and collecting it all with practiced grace.

Ella has since passed, too. She was part of the business from the beginning – the anchor who steadied it through decades of change. A photo of her and Rosie hangs in more than one spot on the walls. It's a quiet reminder that their presence still fills the room, carried on in the people, the place, and the food.

Our barbecue was ready, and we left with a thank you and a tip. Outside we walked to the left of the store and towards the giant metal smokehouse. There were a few empty picnic tables out front – they've since added a large outdoor seating area. We claimed one on the far left of the structure's front door, and a

EMPLOYEES
ONLY

group of employees sat two tables down laughing and talking, probably taking a break from the heat inside. The barbecue was great, as expected. The food matched the way that Scott's presented itself – pragmatic and straightforward. It showcased the pork without trying to cover it up with sauce – essentially avoiding the proverbial lipstick and unabashedly letting the pork speak for itself. The sides were solid and only helped lift the main course. The lidded styrofoam trays were the perfect vessel for the portions and made clean up easy. Nearby, there were more styrofoam boxes being handed out to customers through a side door. We surmised that if you call ahead, you can "come around back" to pick up your meal. This is the local's secret.

I stood up to throw my box away and tried to take a peek inside a window of the smokehouse. There was signage stating that employees were the only ones allowed inside, so I figured I could snap a picture through the window. When I started going for my camera, one of the employees in a red apron that was sitting at the table across from us, told me to go on inside if I liked.

So, I did.

Inside, there was a concrete floor with a 10-foot wide aisle straight down the middle of the Quonset hut that went to the back. Through the smoky haze you could make out another screened door that led out to where the wood piles were. Along each side of the aisle were two long rows of cinder block pits with hogs in various stages of cooking on top of each one. It smelled amazing and was really hot, probably 10-15 degrees warmer than outside – this was a giant smoker after all. The man who invited me in came up behind me at that point and offered to show me through. He said the pits on the right were for large hogs, 250 lbs

Top image: The inside of the smoky smokehouse
Bottom image: My guide stirring the sauce pot. It was really nice
of him to pose for this very touristy photo op by yours truly.

or more, and the ones on the left fit two average hogs on them. Average is 100 to 150 pounds, he said. All I could imagine was the workout they must've gotten moving these animals in and out of here all day.

We made our way through the smoke and out the back door. Right in front of me were two gigantic burn barrels. Old petroleum tanks about six feet tall and three to four feet in diameter. They had rods extruding through the middle from one side to another. The sides of the barrels were warped due to the intense and constant heat. There were rectangular cutouts below the rods near the ground revealing piles of hot coals. Wood was thrown in the top of the barrels and burned. The coals fell to the bottom. They were then hand-shoveled and brought into the smokehouse to evenly distribute under the hogs. My host pointed to the piles of wood and said that he cuts down all of the trees, splits and burns the wood, then brings it in to cook. I told him, "man, that's so much manual labor." He gave me a quizzical look, and I followed up with, "but it's worth it, that's the best barbecue I've ever had." He smiled really big. It was the truth, and I was happy that I could share it with the person that made it.

We walked back through the smokehouse and he showed me where they cook the barbecue sauce – two giant pots with a wooden paddle used for stirring. He stood with one of the pots and posed for a picture. I would have loved to sit down and hear his life story, but I didn't want to overstay my impromptu welcome – he was working after all. After he dropped some hints that they may be eyeing Greenville for a new location – an amazing tidbit of information – I thanked him for his time and walked back outside. In the excitement of the moment, I completely forgot to ask his name. I hope that when I go back I'll see him again, and make a proper introduction.

We hopped back in the car and started on the long trek home. This time, we avoided the flooded highways and had an uneventful drive. As I drove, I couldn't help but reflect on the experience. We went down there for a plate of barbecue and came back with something rarer: a genuine connection to a cuisine – and to the people behind it. The word authenticity comes to mind, before social media deflated the term with curated lifestyle imagery. Scott's in Hemingway makes great barbecue and knows how to show someone a good time.

It's also a place built on layers – of history, of smoke, of stories passed down and tacked on. Each time I visit, new layers appear: a sign added, a memory honored, a face missing, another stepping in. But the barbecue stays the same, anchoring it all. That's the thread – the thing that pulls you back and holds it together.

"The wood that you use has to be right."
—Jaime Jones

→ HOGS,
PIGS &
SWINE

WHERE THE HOGS COME FROM

One of the questions I asked in my interviews for this research was how to go about barbecuing a pig. Robert Moss went into a lot of detail, starting from the beginning:

> *It's not easy to get your hands on a pig. You've got to know where to go... I actually think I list in my book a couple of places in the Carolinas that you can get them, but you've really got to know a meat market. You're not going to be able to go down to the grocery store and order one. I imagine specialty butchers with their connections could probably get you some. But these here in Charleston are mostly getting their pigs from a processing plant up in Kingstree, which is near Hemingway, but that's where Rodney and his family get all their hogs from...Or you could know a farmer. I know a couple of hog farmers who are friends. I can get them from them, but they all go to the same processing plant.*

That being said, a processor is not a farmer. They're one step removed. They take pigs from the farm and prepare them in ideal ways for the end customer to use them. It's a rare thing as a layman to know a pig farmer as Robert does – rarer than it is to find a processor. As I moved deeper in my research and tried to discover where barbecue restaurants acquired their pigs, it was a difficult nut to crack. This wasn't because anyone was trying to hide anything. It was more due to the fact that it wasn't on their radar as something to be concerned about.

Jaime Jones mentioned that when he was in college, he acquired his hogs in a unique way:

" *Clemson used to sell you pigs from the farm up there if they would have a hernia. For some reason they couldn't do whatever they were doing with them so you could go up there and get cheap pigs. But they were live. I mean, you can get a whole pig for like 30 or 40 bucks. We would go up there and get them and come home and kill them and gut them, dehair them and all that at the house. But I don't think they do that anymore, honestly, and I'm too old and lazy probably to do that anyways. I would just buy one. I don't care where it [comes from] – I mean, I've never had one of those Ossabaw pigs or whatever that Sean Brock[50] talks about.*

As unusual as this story is – the more common being along the lines of Robert Moss' explanation – the sentiment of not necessarily being concerned about where the hog came from is typical. In the grand scheme of local culture, barbecue has been around a lot longer than the farm-to-table movement. In all fairness, barbecue has also been around a lot longer than

---

50. Sean Brock is a James Beard award winning chef who made his name in Charleston. Anthony Bourdain called him one of the most important chefs in America. His first cookbook, *Heritage*, is all about embracing the foodways of the Lowcountry.

industrial farming. The lobbying powers of "big ag" have done a really thorough job at covering up the disturbing farming practices of the worst swine farms.[51] In my early research of barbecue, I found myself diving down a deep rabbit hole centered around industrial agricultural practices and the injustice of it all. Not only to the animals, but to the local farmers, purveyors, the environment, and people who end up consuming the products. South Carolina has learned a lot from the errors of North Carolina, so the articles that I read mostly referred to our northern neighbor. The following information is shared for clarity as to why industrial pig farming should be a concern.

North Carolina has the same number of pigs as they have people,[52] and the farms are concentrated in the rural southeastern areas of the state. This is probably why the majority of farms in South Carolina are in the Pee Dee region, almost like they're seeping across the border.[53] These Concentrated Animal Feeding Operations (CAFOs) are known for treating the animals like cogs in a machine. In a modern CAFO, pigs are essentially piled on top of each other inside buildings and are closed off to the outside. They are fed antibiotics in their daily regimen in order to ward off disease. This is because otherwise, these conditions would not be survivable due to the close quarters. Many of the pigs that die are left dead on the ground of the facility and are sent to a rendering plant to be ground into food that is fed back to other pigs.

The animal waste is also an environmental hazard. Emily Moon stated in an article that she wrote for *Pacific Standard* magazine, "With millions of hogs comes a lot of waste. In these giant

---

51. Estabrook, *Pig Tales*. The entirety of Estabrook's book is essentially
    about the farming practices of industrial swine farms.
52. USDA, *2019 State Agricultural Overview, North Carolina*
53. SCDHEC, *Maps of Permitted Agricultural Facilities*

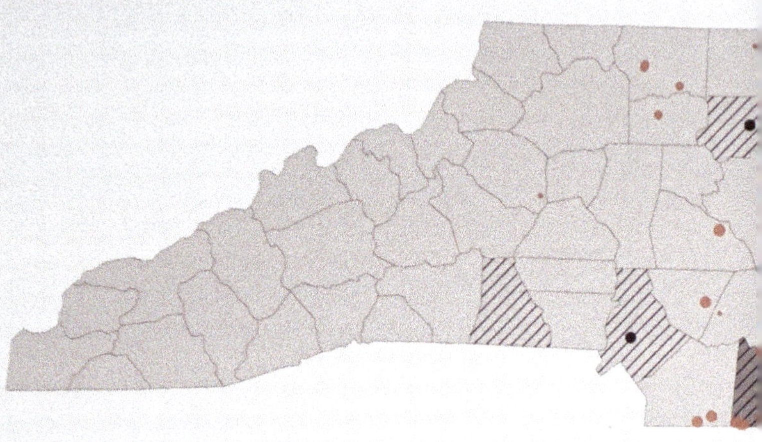

NORTH CAROLINA SWINE CAFOS *and* RACIAL INEQUALITY

African Americans are more than 1.5 times more likely than whites to live within three miles of an industrial hog operation in North Carolina. Latinos and Native Americans are also more likely to live near CAFOs.[54] The members of surrounding communities cannot go outside their houses on days that CAFOs are spraying the fields. They have to keep their doors and windows closed.[55]

The concentration of millions of pigs in southeastern North Carolina is made possible by racial injustices that deny people basic rights.

Steve Wing, an epidemiologist at the University of North Carolina at Chapel Hill, who unfortunately passed away in 2016, stated:

54. Wing, Steve, Jill Johnston, *Industrial Hog Operations in North Carolina*
55. Yeoman, *Complaints about North Carolina's hog pollution*

"*If workers and residents in rural communities that are most directly impacted had basic political and human rights, industrial agriculture would not have developed with such destructive force because those affected by its side effects would have been able to protect themselves.*" [56]

–Steve Wing

56. Wing, *Community Health Impacts of Factory Farms*

operations, feces, urine, and anything else that seeps beneath pens' slatted floors – stillborn pigs, afterbirths, pesticides, blood – form a liquid slurry, which is then pumped into open-earth pits, known in the industry as lagoons."[57] It may be surprising to find out that all of these CAFO farms are surrounded by fields of crops that are used to feed pigs. When the lagoons are full, the slurry is sprayed periodically over these fields under the guise of being fertilizer. "On a continuum of pollutants, it is probably closer to radioactive waste than to organic manure" reported Jeff Tietz of *Rolling Stone*.[58] The runoff from this practice pollutes the groundwater and eventually makes its way back to what we drink.

This is just a small fraction of the reported information on the subject. If you are interested, I implore you to take a look at the plethora of books and documentaries on the matter. Be prepared to have a strong desire to become vegan though. It isn't pretty.

As disturbing as this topic is, the reports around these practices have started to build public knowledge. It probably isn't necessary to mention that the natural habitat of pigs does not include antibiotics and lagoons, unless they're using them to take a bath. The Ossobaw pigs[59] that Jaime mentioned in his comments are a good example of the fact that people are becoming aware of other options that exist. There are farms that raise heritage hogs in more natural habitats that in turn create happier animals and ideally better tasting pork – at least the person consuming it can feel better about it. In fact, in researching the processing plant that Robert mentions, Williamsburg Packing Co., I discovered that it is an Animal

57. Moon, Emily. *North Carolina's Hog Waste Problem*
58. Tietz, Jeff. *Boss Hog: The Dark Side of America's Top Pork Producer*
59. This is a heritage species of hog that Sean Brock talks about in his cookbook *Heritage*. They are direct descendants of the Iberian hogs that Spain brought over in the 16oos. Brock, *Heritage*, 126

Lagoon Facts

60,000 hogs per facility

Serving Size 3 lagoons

Amount per 1 cup

Calories 0

		% Daily Value*
Total Excrement	7g	**17%**
Urine	3g	
Feces	4g	
Body Parts	4	**10%**
Pesticides	300mg	**65%**
Post-Gestation Debris	30g	**8%**
Stillborn pigs	20g	
Afterbirths	10g	
Blood	100g	

Side-Effects due to Exposure

Incresed infant morality rates

Anemia deaths

Kidney disease

Tuberculosis

Asthma

Elevated blood pressure

Sleep disruptions

Depression

Side-Effects due to Ingestion

Death

* Percent Daily Values are generalizations based on the waste that is pumped into the waste lagoons of most CAFO facilities in the United States.

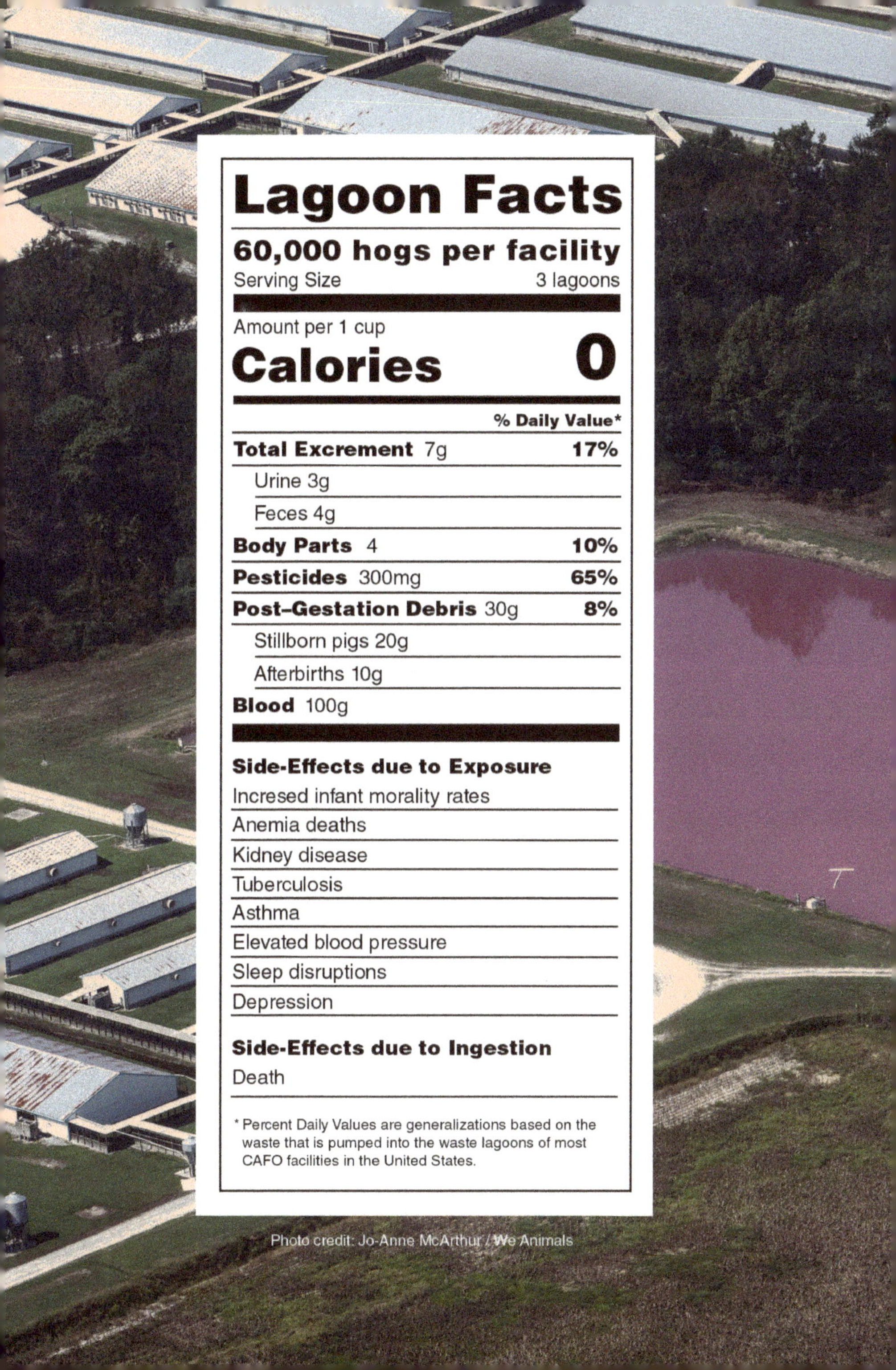

Photo credit: Jo-Anne McArthur / We Animals

Welfare Approved and Certified Humane slaughter facility. This essentially means all of the bad stuff mentioned above is not an issue with the meat that they sell, and consequently with their customer's products. *The Charleston City Paper* reported that people travel upwards of three and a half hours to purchase meat from this processor because of the attention they pay to their meat.[60]

This growing awareness of ethical farming practices is a testament to people dedicated to bringing these injustices to light. In the world of barbecue, the fact that it is becoming more mainstream brings more customers, and in turn, a larger demand for the knowledge of where the meat comes from. Whether or not you are in favor of the mainstreaming of traditional barbecue culture, this is definitely something positive that has come from it. In my research for this project, I have certainly become more aware of these practices, and take notice when the restaurants I visit talk about them in their marketing material. In the end, it drives how I spend my money, and I imagine that I am not the only person who feels this way.

 60. Kelley, *Finding a good butcher can mean a 460-mile round trip*

THE LOWCOUNTRY

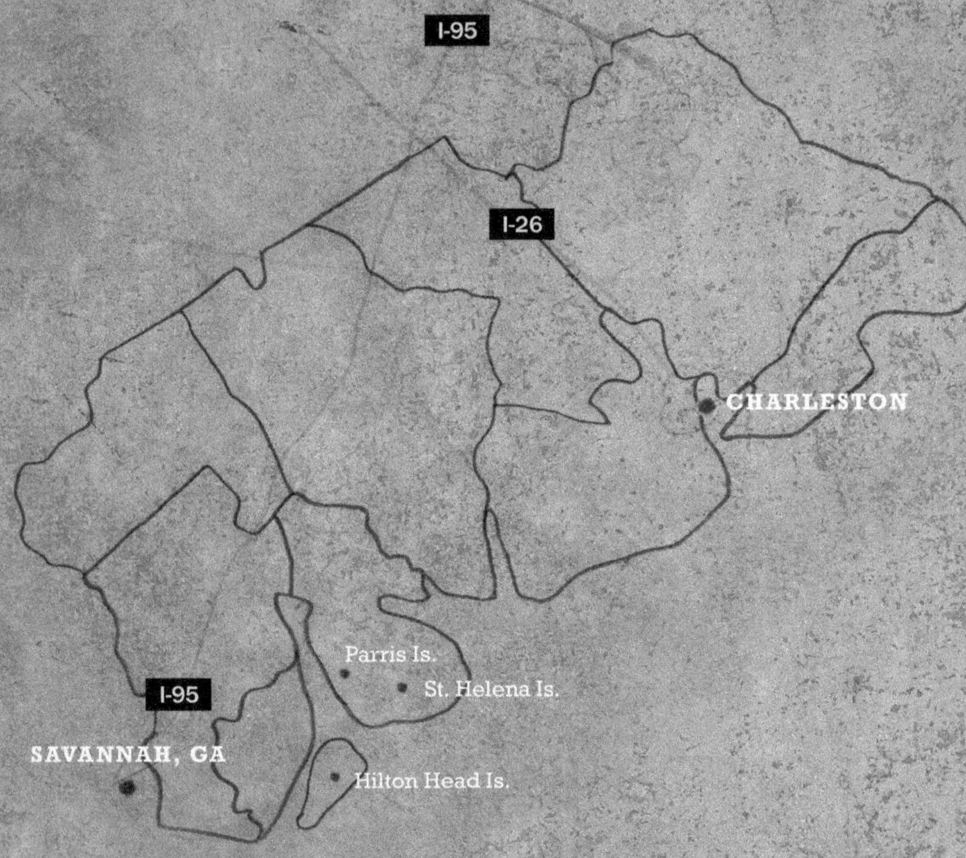

The LOWCOUNTRY REGION
of SOUTH CAROLINA

The Lowcountry is known for southern charm, spanish moss, and some really nice golf courses. Charleston is the heart of the region, and the barbecue follows suit. The city has become a melting pot of the state's cuisine, and vistors travel from all over the world to sample its wares.

OVERVIEW

Charleston. It's the heart of what South Carolinians call the Lowcountry. The region as a whole includes the counties at the bottom of the triangle and extends out into the barrier islands of the Atlantic. This is where you'll find all of the oak-lined roads with Spanish moss hanging off the branches. It gets super humid in the summertime, but there are beautiful beaches to frequent on the days that are unbearable.

The Lowcountry is one of the most visited areas in South Carolina, and for good reason. It's rich in history, and Charleston has a historic district that rivals any in the United States. The southern aristocracy makes its home here and helps support events like the world-famous Spoleto music festival, golf tournaments, and one of the biggest little food scenes in the country. Chefs like the Lee Brothers and Sean Brock[61] have put Charleston on the map with their remaking of southern cuisine into fine culinary experiences – while still retaining the unique character of the region.

---

61. Brock now resides in Nashville, but had an unforgettable impact on the Charleston food scene.

Believe it or not, barbecue has only become a recent point-of-focus in the Lowcountry. Before the last fifteen years, the area was essentially seen as an extension of the Midlands as far as the style of the cuisine. Many of the restaurants that had started further up the state made their way down into the city with their mustard-based sauce. In the last decade, things started to change. There are some newcomers that have started challenging the status quo. For starters, they don't just serve barbecue – they serve salads, alcohol, and entrees other than smoked pork. Basically everything that you would expect from a sit-down dining experience.

Rodney Scott moved to Charleston, leaving the original Hemingway shop under the watchful eye of his family, and started what may soon become an empire of barbecue establishments across the Deep South. John Lewis moved all of the way from Austin, TX to set up Lewis Barbecue a few blocks away from Scott's. Both are leaders in the field, and maybe that is why this is a major part of the food scene in the city now. National credentials go a long way in building a reputation and respect in a city that prides itself on its leadership in high-minded southern cooking.

The barbecue establishments that already existed in the city have been elevated because of these two giants moving in. The Bessinger clan has a couple of places nearby (two of Maurice's brothers) that have been around for years. They're highly rated in terms of the barbecue, and well known because of the name.

This essentially makes Charleston a new hub for the cuisine in the state, as it represents the local history of the food in a walking-tour-style tourist jaunt. It's the place to be for antebellum architecture, Civil War history, and now an overview of the state's barbecue.

NORTH CENTRA
King St
St
BEGIN
CULTURE
SHIFT
WALKING
TOUR

ADD
THE
POPE

THE HOLY TRINITY...AND HASH

Barbecue enthusiasts are pretty serious about their pursuits, to the point where the idea of barbecue as religion has become somewhat of a cliché. That hasn't stopped The Holy Trinity from Christian doctrine making its way into popular barbecue vernacular.

The Holy Trinity is no stranger to culinary reference. The one I am familiar with outside of barbecue refers to onions, bell peppers, and celery in Cajun cuisine. This is due to their inclusion in staple dishes like jambalaya, crawfish étouffée, and gumbo. Whether or not this influenced the use of the term in barbecue is unknown to me, but I can't help but imagine that it was something of an inspiration.

In the Carolinas, The Holy Trinity of barbecue refers to the side dishes of coleslaw, baked beans, and potato salad. To be clear, it does not reference variations of the dish itself, as Texas barbecue enthusiasts proclaim in brisket, ribs, and sausage. It is highly unusual for any barbecue establishment in South Carolina to not include all three of these sides on the menu. Even the bare bones setup of Scott's barbecue in Hemingway offers them in addition to a slice of white bread with every order.

There are variations of each side throughout North and South Carolina. There is a red slaw with vinegar as a base, as well as a creamy slaw that is preferred in some parts. There are as many varieties in potato salad and baked beans as well. The key is that they're included. Other items would be white bread (as in what is mentioned with Scott's above), or hushpuppies, a ball of fried cornmeal batter. Notice that I didn't say cornbread. That's not a typical barbecue side. I'm betting it's because it's a bit too dry to eat with this type of meal.[62]

Once the main three side requirements are met, restaurants go all over the map with their options. From collard greens at Rodney Scott's in Charleston, to sweet potato casserole at Henry's in Greenville. Variations on the classic macaroni and cheese is a popular addition you can find at almost any establishment as well.

One additional side that is absolutely unique to South Carolina is hash. In New Orleans they call the addition of garlic to the trinity "adding the Pope." I imagine that is what hash and rice would be in South Carolina barbecue… adding the Pope.

Hash is traditionally made from all of the extra bits of the pig that can't go in the pit. Kind of like hot dogs, but soupy. It's a common

---

62. A giant exception to this that I know of is the famous Skylight Inn in Ayden, North Carolina where the Jones family runs things. Their presentation is always chopped pork on the bottom, a piece of cornbread in the middle, and a dish of coleslaw on the top. It is delicious, and worth the pilgramage. There are probably other places in the area that serve it with cornbread, but it doesn't seem very common around here.

Barbecue side combinations. On top is Scott's Bar-B-Que in Hemingway. The middle is Piggie Park. On the bottom is Henry's Smokehouse.

"It's like a thick MEAT GRAVY"

—Robert Moss

side dish in the Midlands and the Lowcountry and some places will mix some mustard sauce into it, giving it a yellow tinge. It's commonly confused (at least in Georgia) with Brunswick Stew, but they are decidedly different dishes as hash is pretty much all meat. No stewy vegetables (with the exception of potatoes) are generally added. Hash is served over rice in the Midlands, and is always an accompaniment to barbecue, not a meal unto itself.

Hash is also available in the Upstate and is "linked to the transition of the region's economy from rural agriculture to textile manufacturing."[63] Hash creation moved from farms to mill villages. A lot of mills had a hash house associated with them. Essentially, these were little one-room houses with a big iron pot that had hash cooking in it all day to sell to locals. It was thick and stew-like – typically made with beef rather than pork since it was easier to purchase – and was eaten as a meal unto itself. These houses eventually were squeezed out due to DHEC closing them down. Small shacks with screens for walls wasn't really considered sanitary, but the traditional side continues to be made at restaurants throughout the state, although not in the quaint hash houses of the past.

The only downside to South Carolina's barbecue side options are the typical way they are served. The standard container that is handed out at restaurants for internal dining as well as to-go ordering is the three-way styrofoam plate. This leaves the barbecue enthusiast room for barbecue and two sides, not three, four, or five. It means that the trinity is not a very convenient set of additions to order in one sitting – guaranteeing that you will be back again. I wonder if this was marketing consideration by barbecue entrepreneurs? Texas and New Orleans should take note. Whether the Carolinas started *the holy trinity* naming trend or not, they are most definitely the ones profiting from it.

63. Moss, *Barbecue Lover's The Carolinas*, 154

→ THE
HERE
AND
NOW.
EVERY
DAY

CHARLESTON'S MEATHACKING DISTRICT

The meathacking district is a cute name. I first noticed it when reading a review in the *Charleston City Paper* by Robert Moss.[64] It's an area outside the historical city center that has been collecting barbecue restaurants over the last few years. It wasn't really intentional, it seems like the stars aligned on price per square foot, space required (for the pit houses), and the zeitgeist of barbecue revival. To be fair, Home Team BBQ is pushing for the area to be called Charleston Barbecue District in the form of a hashtag, but I like #meathacking better. Neither seems to have caught on.

64. Moss, James, *Is Charleston the future of Barbecue?*

This is the area my dad and I found ourselves in when we drove into Charleston on a Wednesday close to lunchtime. We were dumped off of I-26 and turned right onto King Street. This street runs parallel to another road called Meeting Street. In my limited experience with Charleston over the years, I've learned that you can get onto either of these streets, drive towards the water, and eventually end up where you want to be. Whether that is a hotel, a fantastic restaurant, or on an old south historical walking tour from the Revolutionary War onward. I learned at an early age not to talk about the fact that my great great great great uncle was William Tecumseh Sherman.[65] People are still bristly about that kind of stuff around here.

It was in the 60s, a highly unusual temperature for mid-June. I was honestly relieved. It made the idea of eating barbecue outside actually sound like a good idea. The humidity can sometimes feel like you're walking through a hot, wet blanket. We drove about a half a mile down King Street and pulled off to the right to park in a Food Lion grocery store parking lot. Rodney Scott's Whole Hog BBQ was across the street and didn't have any free spaces – this was the next best thing. Both of us got out of the car and started walking towards the entrance. Winston (my brother-in-law) and Jaime Jones (one of the barbecue experts that I interviewed for this research) met us there. They were at the beach with their families, so we all decided to meet up and partake in a brief barbecue tour of Charleston.

The restaurant was a low-slung building that had wrap-around glass windows in the front and a patio that did the same – bordered by planters. It could have been a renovated diner from the 50s or

IT'S ALL WOOD
RS

STOP
NO
LEFT
TURN

60s. I learned that the previous inhabitant was a fried chicken restaurant. I'm not sure what it was before that. Since this is Charleston, it's a safe bet to assume there was always something before. It was entirely made of brick that had been painted white with baby blue trim[66] around the windows and flat roof. On the side of the building we were on, next to the side entrance, there was a silhouette of a hog painted on the wall with the letters R and S inside of it. Spelled out above the hog in the shape of a rainbow was the phrase:

IT'S ALL WOOD

This is a phrase that has been attributed to Rodney Scott for years. It's referencing the fact that the flavor of his barbecue comes from the wood he burns – hickory, pecan, and oak.[67] In Hemingway, they collect wood from around the area to make the coals for the pits. This is such a large part of the process that Rien Fertel commented, "if Rodney Scott ever found it necessary to carry a business card, his occupation should read: 'Scott's Bar-B-Que Owner, Professional Pitmaster, and Amateur Arbor-ist'."[68] This was written before Rodney had moved to Charleston to start this business. I'll bet he has a business card now.

The building was pretty swanky, and a far cry from the small build-ing in Hemingway where he cut his teeth. We walked inside and there were 12" diameter globe pendant lights hanging from the ceiling. There was a disco ball spinning awkwardly in the middle of the room as well. I'm not sure if this was permanent, but it was the only piece that reminded me of the layers of change from the original variety store. It also showed a bit of a sense of humor in a location that is unapologetically designed to populate

---

66. A very clear call-out to Scott's Bar-B-Que in Hemingway.
67. In Hemingway this is mostly pecan and oak since hickory is hard to come by. I'm not sure if it's the same in Charleston.
68. Fertel, *The One True Barbecue*, 178

visitors' social media accounts. It was tastefully trendy – you could definitely see it being featured in the fancy food columns of a town that is consistently judged as a top ten food city in the country[69] – that's what is pretty special about this place. The food hasn't changed. Rodney Scott still makes the traditional Pee Dee whole-hog barbecue with vinegar and pepper sauce, but surrounded by a more progressive and modern atmosphere – another option for those that don't want to drive to the middle-of-nowhere for their barbecue fix. But that may come at the expense of authenticity, something worth examining.

This is a quintessential example of the bird leaving the nest and becoming more successful in doing so. There are rumors of animosity in Rodney's hometown – locals disappointed that he left and sold out. But, there's also the perspective that he has found a way to keep the tradition and technique of cooking alive and thriving. Of all of the books I've read about barbecue, that is one opinion that is shared throughout – that whole-hog barbecue was a dying art form, at least until now.

In my discussion with Rien Fertel, I asked him about this transition to larger commercial ventures, and he said the following about Rodney Scott and Sam Jones out of North Carolina (who has done something similar):

For me, I see Scott's Bar-B-Que in Hemingway owning nostalgia, showcasing the way things have always been done. There's no need to change something that works so well. Rodney Scott's Whole Hog Barbecue in Charleston dusts off nostalgia and looks ahead. It still is honoring the methods of the past while catering to the modern mid-scale dining experience expectations. This is

 69. Sietsema, *The 10 Best Food Cities in America, Ranked*

" So [in order to survive] they've had to change the business model by becoming 'real restaurants', and that's what Sam has done, and Rodney Scott has done. Real restaurants that serve salads, and hamburgers, and alcohol, and have air conditioning, stuff like that.

I would never say that what Sam or Rodney has done as owners of their own restaurants, coming from family restaurants, is in any way a diminished product, or a bastardized version. I think it can't help but be better. They're using better products. They are serving a larger customer base. They're still doing the same thing. I mean, it's still whole-hog. It's the same thing. They're not just cooking shoulders like some.

For them to have this dream, and have it come to fruition is such a beautiful thing. Some people say it is a bastardized product. Some people say it is a diminished taste. Some people swear the new places away. They would never eat at those places, and that they've gotten too big for their britches, or whatever it is, and that's just nonsense. "

EVERY DAY
IS A GOOD DAY
Belly Down
— LOW AND SLOW —
42:24
Best Way
KEEPS
6

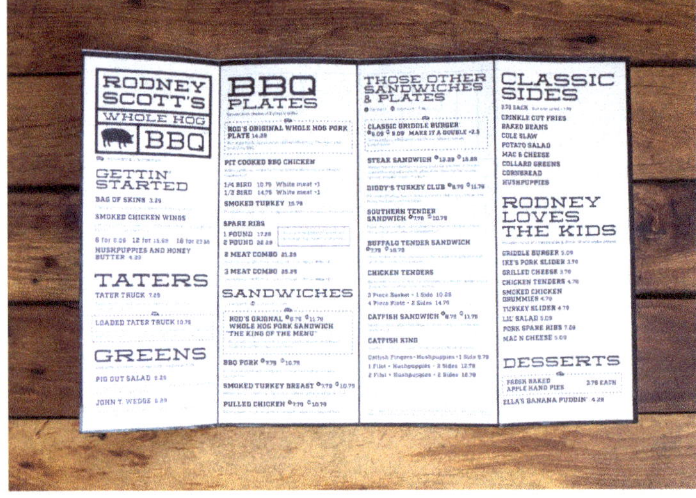
RODNEY SCOTT'S
WHOLE HOG
BBQ

GETTIN' STARTED
BAG OF SKINS 3.29
SMOKED CHICKEN WINGS
6 for 8.09   12 for 15.99   18 for 23.99
HUSHPUPPIES AND HONEY BUTTER 4.29

TATERS
TATER TRUCK 7.69
LOADED TATER TRUCK 10.79

GREENS
PIG OUT SALAD 9.29
JOHN T. WEDGE 8.29

BBQ PLATES
ROD'S ORIGINAL WHOLE HOG PORK PLATE 14.29
PIT COOKED BBQ CHICKEN
1/4 BIRD   10.79   White meat +1
1/2 BIRD   14.79   White meat +1
SMOKED TURKEY 15.79
SPARE RIBS
1 POUND   17.29
2 POUND   38.29
2 MEAT COMBO 21.29
3 MEAT COMBO 25.29

SANDWICHES
ROD'S ORIGINAL   8.79   11.79
WHOLE HOG PORK SANDWICH
"THE KING OF THE MENU"
BBQ PORK   7.79   10.79
SMOKED TURKEY BREAST   7.79   10.79
PULLED CHICKEN   7.79   10.79

THOSE OTHER SANDWICHES & PLATES
CLASSIC GRIDDLE BURGER   8.09   9.09   MAKE IT A DOUBLE +2.5
STEAK SANDWICH   12.29   15.89
DIDDY'S TURKEY CLUB   8.79   11.79
SOUTHERN TENDER SANDWICH   7.79   10.79
BUFFALO TENDER SANDWICH   7.79   10.79
CHICKEN TENDERS
3 Piece Basket · 1 Side 10.29
4 Piece Plate · 2 Sides 14.79
CATFISH SANDWICH   8.79   11.79
CATFISH KING
Catfish Fingers · Hushpuppies · 1 Side 9.79
1 Filet · Hushpuppies · 2 Sides 12.79
2 Filet · Hushpuppies · 2 Sides 16.79

CLASSIC SIDES
3.29 EACH
CRINKLE CUT FRIES
BAKED BEANS
COLE SLAW
POTATO SALAD
MAC & CHEESE
COLLARD GREENS
CORNBREAD
HUSHPUPPIES

RODNEY LOVES THE KIDS
GRIDDLE BURGER 5.09
IKE'S PORK SLIDER 3.79
GRILLED CHEESE 3.79
CHICKEN TENDERS 4.79
SMOKED CHICKEN DRUMMIES 4.79
TURKEY SLIDER 4.79
LIL' SALAD 5.09
PORK SPARE RIBS 7.29
MAC N CHEESE 5.09

DESSERTS
FRESH BAKED APPLE HAND PIES   3.79 EACH
ELLA'S BANANA PUDDIN' 4.29

definitely selling out. But, there is a place for both – and frankly, the new may help create enthusiasts who will eventually seek out the old. Everybody wins.

There was a counter at the back of the main dining room where we placed our order. Above the counter was a slatted chalkboard. Typically this area would be reserved for the menu, but here there was a large slogan that read:

EVERY DAY IS A GOOD DAY

This was written in chalk, but letterforms that matched the branding were used, rather than someone's handwriting. This detail reveals the intentionality behind the whole outfit. They obviously want to play off of the nostalgia inherent in the signage of old-school barbecue joints, but also want to come across as a modern, brand-conscious establishment that belongs in a swanky food scene. On either side of the slogan were tenets of Rodney Scott's with chalk illustrations, sayings like "it's all wood," and "low and slow." These seem to attempt to tell the process and mix it with a story – like a bulleted blog post that is long enough to share a memorable quip, but short enough so as not to lose the viewers' attention. All of these elements wrap the intended experience in a nice package but it's a bit too manufactured to resonate, at least with me. For me, it's knowing Rodney's story and the fact that underneath this sharable surface he's still doing things the way he's always done that makes me want to eat here.

The actual menus were four-fold tabloid-sized sheets that we grabbed while we stood in line. Rien Fertel was right, it was a restaurant. There was definitely barbecue, but also turkey, chicken, catfish and a slew of other offerings, including a kids menu. The biggest change from the back roads of Hemingway was probably the craft beer on tap. This is not something that you would normally see paired with barbecue in South Carolina. But it is a whole new game down in the Holy City. Barbecue has hit the big time, and the public expects a slew of beer options in the sweltering summer Lowcountry heat. That is an income generator that no restaurateur wants to miss out on.

We ordered and found a table outside, where we sat and waited for our food. Our plans were to go to one other place after this, so we just ordered sandwiches (with no sides) in order to save room for the next stop. It was a quiet area alongside the building lined with the planters I noticed as we walked in. There was a hint of smoke in the air wafting up from the pit house at the rear of the main building. You never forgot where you were, even though it may not visually match what you normally expect with that aroma.

The pit house was a separate building, like a traditional pit house. I noticed there was a wood pile around back as well, but the burn barrels were nowhere in sight. I read that the wood is burned in a fireplace inside, which explains the close to twenty-foot chimney rising off the back roof.

This was to contain the heat so it didn't bother the residential neighbors. Moving into a city means you have to abide by the construction code. I'm impressed that they were able to make it happen.

Image opposite: This exemplifies the similarities and differences between two restaurants. The left is the sauce from Rodney Scott's in Charleston. The right is a bottle of sauce from Scott's Bar-B-Que in Hemingway. Both bottles contain the same sauce.

BBQ SAUCE
RODNEY SCOTT'S
WHOLE HOG
BBQ
RODNEY'S SAUCE
MAKE EVERY DAY
A GOOD DAY
MADE WITH LOVE
FOR PORK, CHICKEN, RIBS OR TURKEY
FAMILY AND TRADITION
12 FL OZ (355 mL)

Our sandwiches were brought right away and the pork on the bun looked very similar to what I had eaten previously in Hemingway. Barbecue is never that photogenic, but as pulled pork goes, Rodney Scott's can hold a nice pose. The biggest difference was that it was served on a quaint metal tray with a real fork. There was extra sauce in a side cup (not that it was really needed), but I noticed they didn't go so far as to serve the course on actual plates. Upscale Charleston be damned, this is still old school barbecue and plates just don't seem right. The pork was everything we expected, perfectly sauced and cooked, with everyone at the table exclaiming it was the best they had ever eaten. It just shows that as long as the proper attention is put on the quality of the product, the package that you wrap it in can be whatever you want it to be.

After about a half hour of chowing down on our sandwiches, we left and made our way over five blocks to the next stop, a Texas barbecue joint. This is a bit of an unusual place to include here, but since I'm talking about how the Lowcountry is looking forward, it shouldn't be skipped. Texas is beef country and their barbecue reflects that. So, it was not a surprise that when we pulled into the parking lot of Lewis Barbecue there was a large mural of a cow's head with a crown that read:

ALL HAIL THE KING

This was a not-so-subtle affront to the region's preferred protein, but judging by how many cars were lined up on the blacktop, the locals didn't seem that offended.

ALL HAIL

THE KING

John Lewis assisted in the early days of the famed Franklin Barbecue in Austin, Texas, before opening his own spot there, La Barbecue. In 2015, he packed up and moved to South Carolina to make his mark in Charleston. The best barbecue in Austin[70] was now in the Lowcountry. Famous for the brisket, the hot guts (sausages), and custom smokers that fill the pit house, it is not South Carolina barbecue, but it is definitely now part of the scene.

We walked across the parking lot, and I noticed the logo for Lewis used a script for the name paired with a nondescript serif typeface to spell out *barbecue*. I thought it was interesting that the guy from Texas doesn't use a western style typeface, but the South Carolina pitmaster down the street uses a slab serif that could be taken right off the hindquarters of a cow. That's a good lesson in public perception and what is considered authentic in the region that you're in. Speaking of authentic, there was a sign with lights hanging on the corner of the building that read:

GET YOUR MEAT *HERE*

It was vertically oriented inside an arrow pointing to the entrance door. This sign was much smaller, but it reminded me of the Vegas style sign that presided over the busy Columbia highway for Piggie Park. This one made a little more sense. After all, Austin is much closer to Las Vegas. American western aesthetic for a western-style cuisine.

Lewis Barbecue was large inside. There was plenty of space for a long line of people (it was not too crowded when we were there). At the front of the line was a long ordering counter that upon closer inspection revealed itself as a butcher station.

  70. Odam, *The best barbecue in Austin, according to Matthew Odam*

That's Winston and Jaime – Winston is wearing the hat.

GET
YOUR
MEAT
HERE

The menu was above the counter. It was professionally printed –
and mounted to a board – using a condensed sans-serif to list all
of the options to order. Mostly, it was meat. There was a large list
of sides – cowboy pinto beans and green chili corn pudding would
be two that aren't typically found on a South Carolina barbecue
menu. I wanted to try the sliced brisket, and either I was too
distracted with studying the new space, or somehow forgot that I
had just eaten a pork sandwich. Either way, the next few moments
were embarrassing, but I don't regret them.

The man behind the counter held up two big briskets (giant hunks
of meat) and informed me that one was the fatty one and the
other was the lean one. He then asked which one I wanted. Of
course, I said the fatty one. Not only did I say the fatty one, but I
asked for half a pound. Half a freaking pound. Now, I think I did
this because the menu said that you could order by the pound,
but I don't think they would've minded if I just said a quarter of a
pound especially since I ordered a link of hot guts. Yup, did that
too. Anyway, I went with it, and the butcher cut two slices from the
big hunk of meat and weighed them. It came out to .7 pounds. My
stomach churned. I paid for everything and took it to the table.
Everyone else had ordered a small chopped brisket sandwich and
laughed pretty hard at me when I sat down.

There were no plates. Everything was laid out on butcher paper
that was served on top of a plastic tray. I'm assuming that this is
how it was done in Texas, and I did not mind. My collard greens,
yes I ordered collard greens in a half-hearted attempt to ingest
some kind of vegetable for the day, were in a small paper board
tray alongside the brisket and sausage. Was it all worth it? Yes.
It was the best brisket I've ever eaten, hands down. Everyone
helped me with the hot guts, thank God.

We sat at a table that overlooked a larger courtyard area covered in live oaks with lights hanging from the branches. The screened-in pit house presided over this part of the restaurant, and it seemed like a place that could handle some pretty big parties. Across the room from our table was a gigantic horseshoe bar. It had an extensive craft beer list and what looked like a full bar with a cocktail program to boot. This was a long ways away from sweet tea and lemonade. After about half an hour, we stood up to head out and left the building underneath the Vegas arrow sign near the entrance.

I couldn't help but think about the fact that right next door was another acclaimed barbecue joint called Fiery Ron's Home Team BBQ, known for its creative takes on the classic cuisine. This place is run by chef Aaron Siegel who is Culinary Institute of America trained. It sounds like a great place to start the transition from acclaimed Charleston cuisine to the more traditional barbecue fare, offering dishes from all over the South and some unique variations like BBQ sliders and nachos.

These three places are pretty close in proximity, but don't compete so much as they complement each other. Elsewhere in Charleston, two sons of Joe Bessinger have restaurants – Melvin's and Bessigner's – that feature the famous Midlands-style mustard sauce so as to ensure that the style South Carolina is famous for is in reach. All of these together make Charleston a one-stop melting pot barbecue extravaganza. The tourists that come to see the last vestiges of the old South don't have to go far to experience a really excellent offering of its oldest cuisine.

I don't see whole-hog barbecue disappearing anytime soon. What does seem to be fading, however, is the unique atmosphere and visual distinctions each region once brought to the table – often replaced by polished branding and photo-ready interiors. In the Lowcountry, this trade-off appears intentional: visual culture gives way to the continuation of a long-standing tradition. For South Carolina pitmasters and proprietors alike, the focus has always been on the product, not the presentation. That priority likely explains why traditional cooking techniques have endured as long as they have – along with the simple fact that they produce excellent barbecue.

We all said our goodbyes and my dad and I made our way back to the car. The drive home was a good three hours, and I was definitely going to skip dinner. It was all worth it, and I look forward to doing it again. Seriously, it was that good. Charleston tends to grab the attention when it comes to our little state, but it does an effective job at raising awareness of southern traditions that may otherwise get lost in the name of progress. Shrimp and grits is a great example. Now, it seems to be garnering national acclaim for the traditions of South Carolina barbecue and giving credit to the pitmasters and innovators where it is due. I suppose I'm okay trading a few hand-made signs and styrofoam plates for that, and I look forward to seeing the roads that this generation leads the cuisine down.

THE
EMBERS

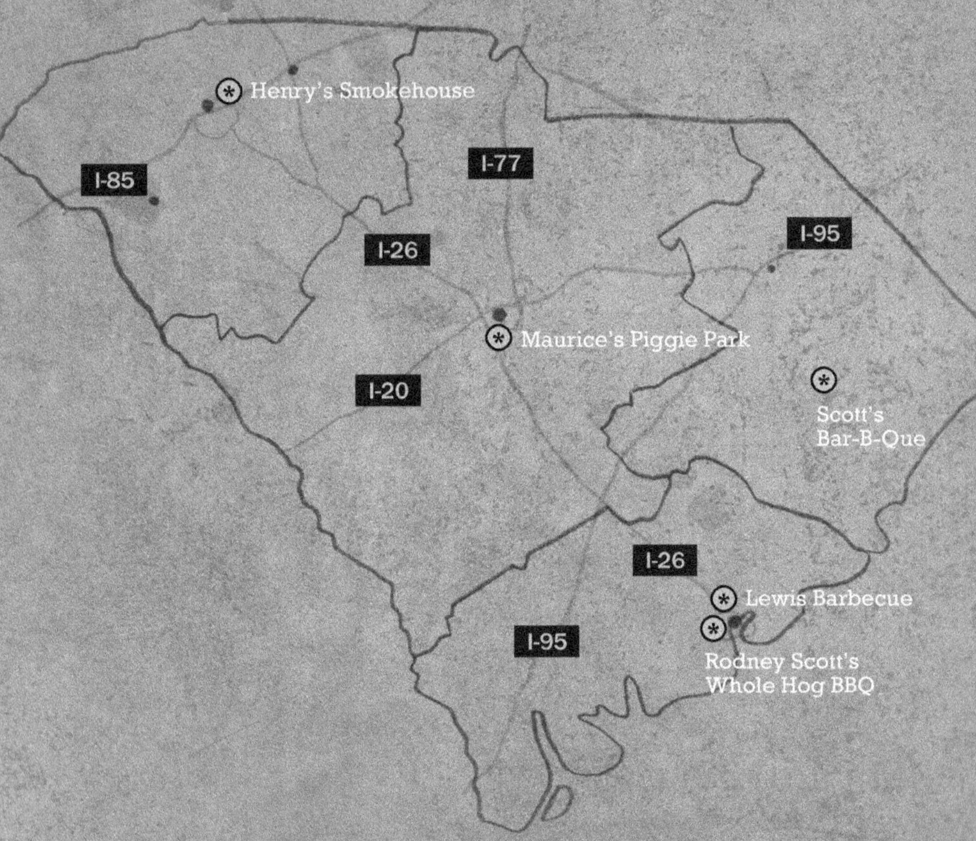

Henry's Smokehouse
I-85
I-77
I-26
I-95
Maurice's Piggie Park
I-20
Scott's
Bar-B-Que
I-26
Lewis Barbecue
I-95
Rodney Scott's
Whole Hog BBQ

The CASE STUDIES
These are the locations of the case study restaurants that
appear throughout this book. They are dispersed, diverse,
and a make up a small slice of a rich culinary and visual
culture that reflect the regions they call home.

CONCLUSION

In my conversation with Rien Fertel, I asked him what came to mind when he thought about barbecue. His initial response was "at one point in my life, I probably would have answered like, 'oh, a sandwich'." I shared the same perspective before I embarked down this complex and winding path of a cuisine that has roots that run incredibly deep in the region of the country that I call home.

This institution is indeed centered around the product of pulled pork, in the form of a sandwich or not. But it is also made up of family legacies, childhood memories, and socio-political rivalries. The visual culture surrounding the cuisine – the long shovels, the burn barrels, the concrete smoky pits – speaks to the hard-working pitmasters of the Pee Dee working for years to perfect what is on the surface a simple recipe, but underneath is a nuanced dish with infinite variables that takes generations to master.

The slick menus and Vegas-style signs speak to the chains of the Midlands and the inevitable commodification of the cuisine, specifically the sauce. It also speaks to how that can turn into a political and cultural lightning rod.

The social media-worthy restaurant layouts and superstar status of the pitmasters in the Lowcountry speak to the future of the cuisine. This future is building whole-hog empires and introducing new generations to something that has been part of the American South since the 1500s. They are ensuring that memory and nostalgia continue to shape the future of barbecue and are building onto a complex and layered culinary identity.

DeSoto had plans to plunder the natural resources of what is now South Carolina when his soldiers overtook the British camp on St. Helena Island. They didn't end up staying for long, but what they left behind, along with the Native American tribes in the area, was the legacy of the first true American cuisine. The legacy still endures today, mirroring the social complexities of the present as it looks back on the turbulent nature of how it came to be. When you think of the South now, I hope you are able to add barbecue to the list along with cornbread, grits, and *y'all.* It has been around a long time, and has the cultural foundation to ride out any storm, emerging stronger on the other side.

  71. Carr, *The Shallows,* 197

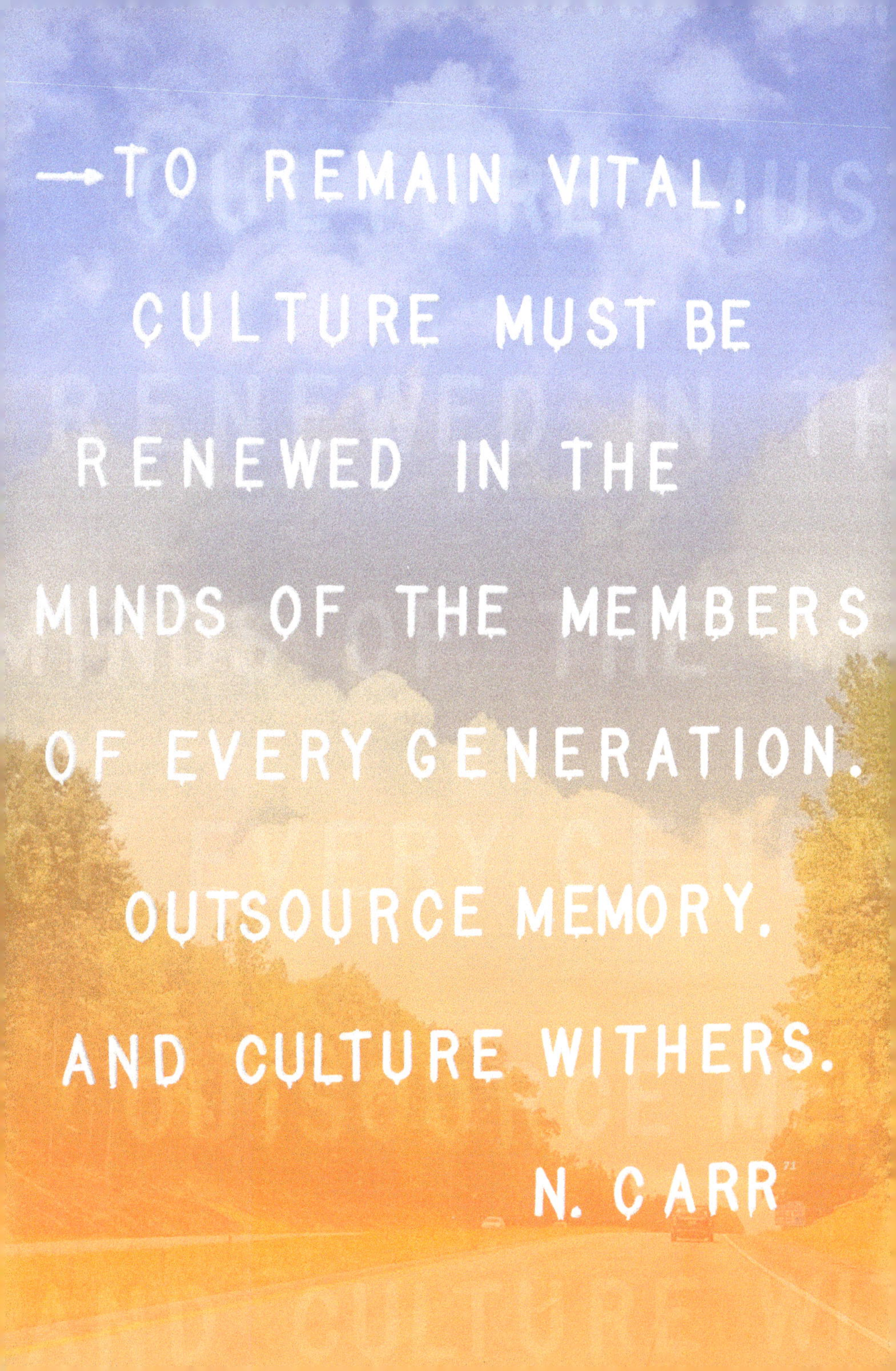

→ TO REMAIN VITAL,
CULTURE MUST BE
RENEWED IN THE
MINDS OF THE MEMBERS
OF EVERY GENERATION.
OUTSOURCE MEMORY,
AND CULTURE WITHERS.
N. CARR

SMOKE
SPRINGS
ETERNAL

EPILOGUE

In the beginning of this research, I set out to
delve into how the visual culture of barbecue
helped reflect and define this institution that has
been around since before the country existed.
I was led down some pretty diverse paths.

The cannibal pig predominance in the identities
still fascinate me. I have developed a new habit
of stopping the car to take pictures of these
signs as I see them on the side of the road
– to the eye-roll annoyance of anyone who is
with me. What can I say?

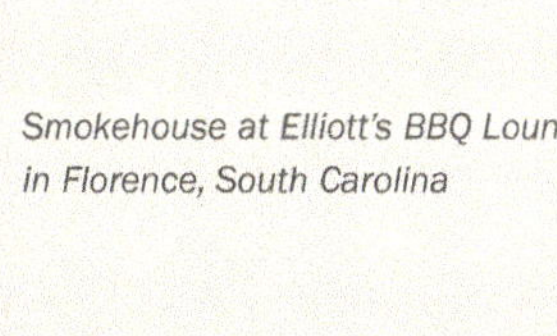

*Smokehouse at Elliott's BBQ Lounge
in Florence, South Carolina*

I became a vegan for three months after I learned about the commercial feeding operations in North Carolina and had to reconcile that within myself to be able to continue writing this book. Now, I continue to eat meat in much smaller quantities and have learned to pay more attention to where my food comes from. Welcome to the 21st century.

I traveled to areas of the state I have never visited before. I learned a lot about the landscape of where I am from. I don't think I would have had the inclination to do that otherwise. Cuisine, place, and culture are intertwined. That concept really hit home through this experience.

I was able to have fascinating conversations with experts on the subject matter, and discovered that they were in the same spot as myself at one point in time. It was a humbling and exciting moment. I also connected with people I've known for years on a topic that neither one of us knew we had in common.

I accomplished my initial goal through the documentation of my personal experiences combined with my interviews and research on all matters of the subject. All of that combined into this package seems to reflect what I was trying to do, but I can't help but want more.

What I discovered throughout this process is that it was not diffi-cult to find topics to explore, what was difficult was determining what to cut out. This was a major factor in my decision to focus on my home state – I could stretch all of what I've done across the whole southeast, and frankly over the entire country.

That being said, here are some of the additional questions
and thoughts that this research has uncovered:

- What about North Carolina? Texas? Kansas City? Memphis?
- What about barbecue that's not in the South?
- Is there a 'right' way to commercialize the cuisine?
- Racial inequality and barbecue are intertwined at important
  moments in history. The study of how this has unfolded
  would be fascinating.
- Barbecue signage – and type usage – across the country.
- How do memory and place relate specifically to the lives of
  the people who grew up around barbecue? To the people
  who own and run the restaurants? To the pitmasters who
  have been doing this their whole lives?
- The new pitmasters – online resources seem to be utilized
  more and more to learn the old techniques of barbecue.
  How has that changed the landscape, especially in the
  regional differences of the cuisine?
- Hash houses. Enough said.
- More tangential to barbecue, but no less interesting in
  terms of visual culture: the meat-and-three style restaurants
  that exist all over South Carolina.
- In addition to the Holy Trinity, are there regional distinctions
  between the common sides that are served?
- The competition circuit is a big deal. How do the different
  regions differ in their judging? How have they helped to put
  their barbecue styles on the map?
- What about Alabama white sauce?[72]

---

72. This last bullet reflects a contribution from the book's editor, Lelia King, who was "born
    and raised [in Alabama] and never heard of this phenomenon [the white sauce] until
    leaving the state."

If you have an interest, I implore and encourage you to take one of these and run. I'm doing the best I can, but the more this topic is explored the more other questions are revealed. This has been a way to explore what some may consider headier subjects through an approachable, and very appetizing, lens.

In the quote from Nicholas Carr that was featured at the beginning of this section, he mentions that "culture must be renewed in the minds of the members of every generation." My thoughts are that this institution is successful when restaurants celebrate the cuisine's diverse history rather than try to cover it up. Commercialization and expansion may be necessary to keep some of the more traditional techniques alive. On one hand, this may be required from a financial perspective, and on the other hand to adapt to changing tastes in younger clientele. Change is part of barbecue's rich past. Embracing change while celebrating the history will inevitably keep the hogs smoking on pits for years to come.

Three smokehouses. The top is Scott's Bar-B-Que, the middle is Maurice's Piggie Park (post fire), and the bottom is Henry's Smokehouse

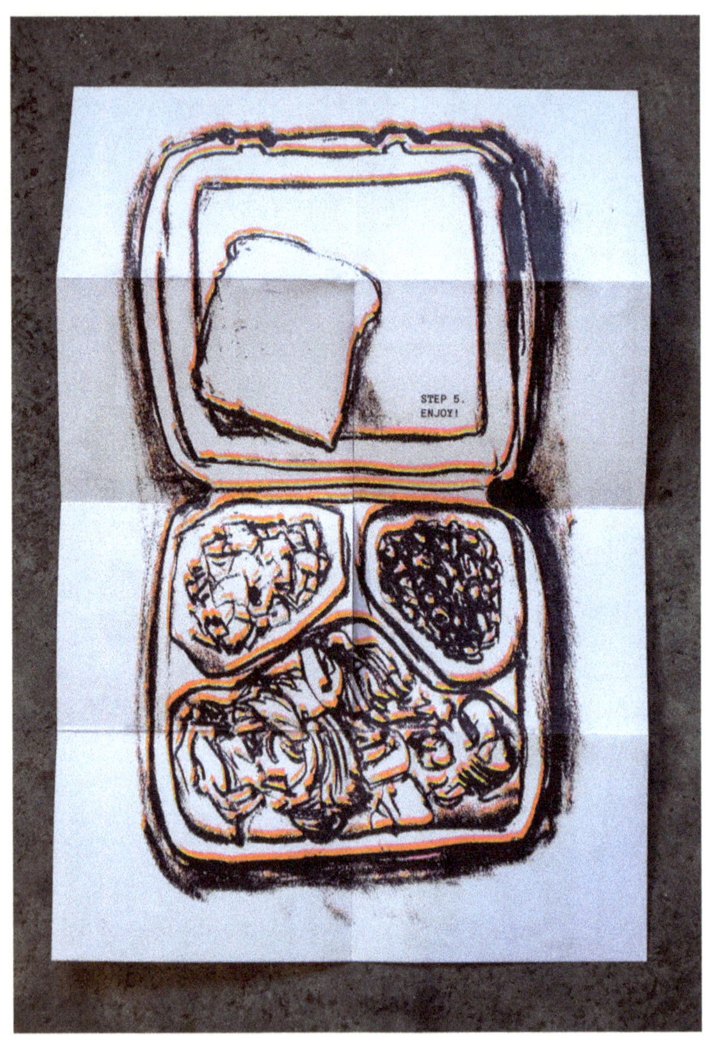

Risograph print of charcoal drawing of plate of Scott's Bar-B-Que, by the author

BIBLIOGRAPHY AND OTHER RESOURCES

Auchmutey, Jim. *Smokelore : A Short History of Barbecue in America.* Athens: University of Georgia Press, 2019.

Berger, John. *Ways of Seeing, Based on the BBC Television Series with John Berger: A Book.* London: BBC, 1972.

Blauvelt, Andrew, Ellen Lupton, Rob Giampietro, Åbäke (Design Studio), and Walker Art Center. *Graphic Design : Now in Production.* 1st ed. Minneapolis, MN: Walker Art Center, 2011.

Brock, Sean. *Heritage.* New York: Artisan, 2014.

Carr, Nicholas G. *The Shallows : What the Internet Is Doing to Our Brains.* 1st ed. New York: W.W. Norton, 2010.

Cepelewicz, Jordana. "The Brain Maps Out Ideas and Memories Like Spaces." *Quanta magazine.* January 14, 2019. https://www.quantamagazine.org/the-brain-maps-out-ideas-and-memories-like-spaces-20190114/

Chau, Danny. "The Soul of Barbecue Is Being Reimagined in Charleston." *The Ringer.* Last accessed October 2025. https://www.theringer.com/2017/08/22/food/soul-of-barbecue-charleston-south-carolina

Collins, Lauren. "America's Most Political Food." *The New Yorker.* Last accessed October 2025. https://www.newyorker.com/magazine/2017/04/24/americas-most-political-food

Estabrook, Barry. *Pig Tales : An Omnivore's Quest for Sustainable Meat.* First ed. New York: W.W. Norton & Company, 2015.

Fertel, Rien, and Denny Culbert. *The One True Barbecue : Fire, Smoke, and the Pitmasters Who Cook the Whole Hog.* New York: Touchstone, 2016.

High, Lake E. *A History of South Carolina Barbeque. American Palate.* Charleston, SC: American Palate, 2013.

High Jr., Lake E. "BBQ History." *South Carolina Barbecue Association.* Last accessed October 2025. https://www.scbarbeque.com/bbq-history/

Howard-Sheridan, Lorena. *Sideway Glances : Vernacular Mexican Lettering.* Author's Edition, 2015 ed. Austin, Texas: Peccata Minuta, 2015.

Kandel, Eric R. *In Search of Memory : The Emergence of a New Science of Mind.* 1st ed. New York: W.W. Norton, 2006.

Kelley, Nikki Seibert. "For heritage-breed farmers, finding a good butcher can mean a 460-mile round trip." *Charleston City Paper.* Last accessed October 2025. https://charlestoncitypaper.com/2015/07/15/for-heritage-breed-farmers-finding-a-good-butcher-can-mean-a-460-mile-round-trip/

Kovacik, Charles F, and John J Winberry. *South Carolina : The Making of a Landscape.* Columbia, SC: University of South Carolina Press, 1989.

Kuo, Andrew, and Kelefa Sanneh. *What Me Worry.* Bologna: Damiani, 2010.

LaRou, George. *"Roadside Culture: Visual Norms and How They Were Established." Lift and Separate: Graphic Design and the Quote Unquote Vernacular.* Edited by Barbara Glauber, pp. 22-29. Princeton, NJ: Princeton Architectural Press, 1996.

Lupton, Ellen, and J. Abbott Miller. *Design Writing Research : Writing on Graphic Design.* London: Phaidon, 1999.

Lupton, Ellen. *"Low and High: Design in Everyday Life." Looking Closer : Critical Writings on Graphic Design.* Edited by Steven Heller, Elinor Pettit and Theodore Gachot, pp. 104-108. New York (N.Y.): Allworth Press, 1994.

Moon, Emily. "North Carolina's Hog Waste Problem Has a Long History. Why Wasn't It Solved in Time for Hurricane Florence?" *Pacific Standard.* Last accessed October 2025. https://psmag.com/environment/why-wasnt-north-carolinas-hog-waste-problem-solved-before-hurricane-florence/

Moser, May-Britt, Rowland, David C., Moser, Edvard I. "Place Cells, Grid Cells, and Memory." *Cold Spring Harbor Perspectives in Biology* 2015;7:a021808. https://cshperspectives.cshlp.org/

Moss, Robert F. *Barbecue : The History of an American Institution.* Tuscaloosa, Alabama: University of Alabama Press, 2018.

Nixon, Sean. *Representation: Cultural Representations and Signifying Practices.* Sage Publications, 2010.

Norman, Donald A. *The Design of Everyday Things. Revised and expanded.* New York, New York: Basic Books, 2013.

Odam, Matthew. "The best barbecue in Austin, according to Matthew Odam." *Austin American-Statesman.* Last accessed October 2025. https://www.statesman.com/story/news/2014/10/29/the-best-barbecue-in-austin-according-to-matthew-odam/10111568007/

Poynor, Rick. *No More Rules : Graphic Design and Postmodernism.* New Haven, CT: Yale University Press, 2003.

Remington, R. Roger, and Lisa Bodenstedt. *American Modernism: Graphic Design 1920 to 1960.* Mini ed. London: Laurence King Publishing, 2013.

Rennie, John. "Artificial Neural Nets Grow Brainlike Navigation Cells." *Quanta magazine.* May 09, 2018. https://www.quantamagazine.org/artificial-neural-nets-grow-brainlike-navigation-cells-20180509/

Roediger, III, Henry L., DeSoto, K. Andrew. "The Power of Collective Memory." *Scientific American.* June 28, 2016. https://www.scientificamerican.com/article/the-power-of-collective-memory/

Rogoff, Irit. "Studying Visual Culture." In *The Visual Culture Reader*, edited by Nicholas Mirzoeff, pp. 24-36. London: Routledge, 1998.

Roller, Jim, and Heather Roller. "SC BBQ Trail Map." *Destination BBQ.* Last accessed October 2025. https://destination-bbq.com/sc-bbq-map-locator/

Rosenberg, and Grafton. *Cartographies of Time.* New York: Princeton Architectural Press, 2010.

Shields, David. "What is Wood Type?" *Hamilton Wood Type & Printing Museum.* Last accessed October 2025. https://woodtype.org/pages/what-is-wood-type

South Carolina General Assembly. House. *Require the Department of Agriculture to design and print decals which may be displayed wherever barbeque is sold.* HR 3718. 106th sess., introduced in House March, 27th 1986. https://www.scstatehouse.gov/sess106_1985-1986/bills/3718.htm

U.S. Congress. House. Uniting and Strengthening America by Providing Appropriate Tools Required to Intercept and Obstruct Terrorism (USA PATRIOT ACT) Act of 2001. HR 3162. 107th Cong.,1st sess. Introduced in House October 23, 2001. https://www.congress.gov/107/plaws/publ56/PLAW-107publ56.pdf

South Carolina Department of Heath and Environmental Control, "Maps of Permitted Agricultural Facilities." SCDHEC. Last accessed July 2020. https://gis.dhec.sc.gov/gis-portal/apps/webappviewer/index.html?id=5748b81cf2d-84668be4175eed2511654

Sturken, Marita, and Lisa Cartwright. *Practices of Looking : An Introduction to Visual Culture.* Third ed. New York: Oxford University Press, 2018.

Tietz, Jeff. "Boss Hog: The Dark Side of America's Top Pork Producer." *Rolling Stone.* Last accessed October 2025. https://www.rollingstone.com/culture/culture-news/boss-hog-the-dark-side-of-americas-top-pork-producer-68087/

Treib, Marc. "Mapping Experience." *Design Quarterly,* no. 115 (1980): 1-32. doi:10.2307/4091019.

Tufte, Edward R, and Graphics Press. *Envisioning Information.* Cheshire, Connecticut: Graphics Press, 1990.

United States Department of Agriculture National Agriculture Statistics Service. "2019 State Agricultural Overview, North Carolina." USDA. Last accessed October 2025. https://www.nass.usda.gov/Quick_Stats/Ag_Overview/stateOverview.php?state=NORTH%20CAROLINA

Venturi, Robert, Denise Scott Brown, and Steven Izenour. *Learning from Las Vegas.* Facsimile ed. Cambridge, Massachusetts: MIT Press, 2017.

Walker Art Center, Cranbrook Art Museum, and Berkeley Art Museum and Pacific Film Archive. *Hippie Modernism : The Struggle for Utopia.* Edited by Andrew Blauvelt. Firsted. Minneapolis: Walker Art Center, 2015.

Wing, Steve. "Community Health Impacts of Factory Farms." *TedX Manhattan 2013*. Last accessed October, 2025. https://youtu.be/7ZW8-LQftnY

Wing, Steve, Jill Johnston. Industrial Hog Operations in North Carolina Disproportionately Impact African-Americans, Hispanics and American Indians. Chapel Hill: The University of North Carolina at Chapel Hill, 2014. Accessed October, 2025. http://www.ncpolicywatch.com/wp-content/uploads/2014/09/UNC-Report.pdf

Wood, Denis, and Ira Glass. *Everything Sings : Maps for a Narrative Atlas.* 1st ed. Los Angeles, CA: Siglio, 2010.

Woodard, Colin. *American Nations : A History of the Eleven Rival Regional Cultures of North America.* New York, NY: Penguin Books, 2012.

Yeoman, Barry. "For years, complaints about North Carolina's hog pollution vanished in state bureaucracy." *Food & Environment Reporting Network.* Last accessed October 2025. https://thefern.org/2019/08/for-years-complaints-about-north-carolinas-hog-pollution-vanished-in-state-bureaucracy/

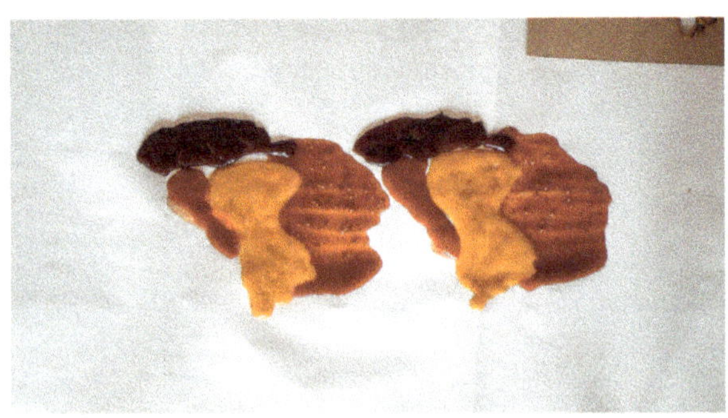

Behind the scenes – making the sauce map was a messy process

INDEX

A

Advertising

See also Branding, Ephemera, Signage

newspaper advertisements 97, 99

regional promotion of barbecue 38, 54, 78, 89, 91, 171

spelling variations of "barbecue" 27

typography in early advertisements 52

Architecture

See also Interiors

barbecue restaurant buildings 48, 49, 83, 86, 110, 132, 160–163, 174, 178, 191

roadside structures 83, 117

B

Barbecue

See also Fire, Foodways

definitions and terminology 8, 9, 16, 29, 30, 83, 95–100

early barbecue practices 27, 28, 44, 77, 95

regional styles in South Carolina 7, 15–16, 33–34, 44, 53, 77, 86–87, 114–115, 127, 150

staples and traditions 15, 27–38, 49, 51, 53, 66–70, 92, 96, 114, 118, 127, 136, 153–157, 177, 180, 189

Barbecue pits 30, 38, 43, 47–49, 114, 122, 132, 134–135, 163, 183, 190, 83, 86, 129, 132, 134, 135

construction methods 27, 132–135

materials used 27, 132

Branding 179

See also Advertising, Ephemera, Signage

hand-painted 9, 34, 47, 59, 90, 95, 122, 126, 163, 171

logos and marks 34, 51, 57, 58–62, 81, 83, 90, 99, 163, 174

modern branding in barbecue restaurants 9, 18, 38, 49, 54, 57–58, 60, 62, 78, 80, 89, 91, 128, 164, 174, 184

RESTAURANTS FEATURED

Name	Region	Pages
Bubba's BBQ & Bash	Upstate	59
Bucky's Bar-B-Q – Greenville	Upstate	39, 58, 61
Circle M BBQ	Upstate	20
City Limits Barbeque	Midlands	36–37, 60
Easton Barbecue Co.	Lowcountry	9
Elliott's BBQ Lounge	Pee Dee	5, 9, 17, 186
Henry's Smokehouse – Greenville	Upstate	42–55, 94, 155, 182, 191
Hite's Bar B. Q.	Midlands	Cover Flap, 6, 59
Home Team BBQ – Greenville	Upstate	58
Lewis Barbecue – Charleston	Lowcountry	147, 171–180, 182
Little Pigs Bar-B-Q – Greenville	Upstate	58
Maurice's Piggie Park	Midlands	71, 76–93, 155, 156, 182, 191
Midway BBQ	Upstate	25, 59, 152
Mike and Jeff's BBQ	Upstate	Cover, 10, 60
Rodney Scott's Whole Hog BBQ – Charleston	Lowcountry	64, 158–171, 182
Scott's Bar-B-Que	Pee Dee	Back Cover, 12–13, 101, 105–138, 155, 181, 182, 191–192
The Smokin' Pig BBQ – Anderson	Upstate	18, 58

ACKNOWLEDGMENTS

This book is dedicated to Jess, my wife and partner. I have no doubt that your unwavering support throughout this project is the primary reason it exists in this form. Thank you forever for your clear head and patient heart. I love you.

Thank you to Robert Moss, Rien Fertel, and Jaime Jones. Your knowledge, input, and time adds a level of depth to this work that could never have been achieved through reading alone. Thank you as well to Robert for writing a foreword that means more to me than you know.

Lib Ramos of Good Printed Things – I'm so grateful you saw potential in this little project. It means the world that you trusted me to see it through to the end. Here's to many more collaborations.

Lelia King, my kindred Southern spirit and editor. I couldn't imagine anyone better to discuss the nuances of Southern culture with. Thank you for your kind words, encouragement, and critique.

Thank you to each of my VCFA advisors: Dave Peacock, Matthew Monk, Lorena Howard-Sheridan, and Silas Munro. Your advice and feedback on my original thesis pushed me to make something I never would have dreamed possible.

Finally, thank you to my family and friends for the company on my many research trips (4 Little Pigs 4EVA), your unflinching encouragement, and your willingness to listen to me drone on for hours on end about barbecue.

COLOPHON

The slab serif that I use for section headers is Rockwell. This typeface was modeled after the 1910 font called Litho Antique created by William Schraubstadter. Morris Fuller Benson revived it in the 1920s and Monotype released this version in 1934 – the project was spearheaded by Frank Hunman Pierpont. Rockwell is incredibly appropriate given the proclivity of barbecue restaurants to choose Antique typefaces in their identities and branding.

The body copy used is ITC Franklin Gothic. The original Franklin Gothic was cut in 1902 and was originally designed by Morris Fuller Benton (same as Rockwell). This iteration added a bit of x-height and character width. It's probably more intended to be used in a larger format – but I appreciate how it pairs with the slab-serif, has strong readability, and shares the same lineage as Rockwell.

Author and Designer: Nathan Spainhour
Editor: Lelia King

All photographs are by the author unless otherwise credited.

Published by Good Printed Things in Greenville, South Carolina.

BAR
BE
QUE
FOREVER
REAL SMOKE
LOW & SLOW